AS WE FIGHT

A Weekly Guide
Through the
Warfare of Worship

MICHAEL LACEY

Aswefightbook.com

FREE FOR ALL!

My gift to you: a free digital download of AS WE FIGHT: A WEEKLY GUIDE THROUGH THE WARFARE OF WORSHIP. Subscribe at aswefightbook.com/ddl to get a free copy! You'll also get updates on future devotionals and writings.

To get some free music, check out my music page, and explore more of my endeavors, check out michaellaceymusic.com. Follow on your preference of social media as well!

As soon as you can, please take some time to leave an honest review for this book on Amazon to help potential readers know what to expect, and keep an eye out (you'll get that joke as you get to know me) for more!

I dedicate this book to those worship leaders who,
like myself, are bi-vocational.

Believe me, I know that it's still a full-time job,
and one of the greatest callings we can have on earth.

TABLE OF CONTENTS

PREFACE

About two years ago, I started working at my church part time, even though I have been leading worship for much longer. To encourage my team members each Sunday morning, I began to reach into God's word, as well as other sources influenced by Him, and He provided creative perspectives and inspiring words. After a while, I began to store them in a note that I called, "As We Fight."

I've always wanted to write a book. We all have burning passions inside that won't be quenched until action is taken. I must create, or I will decay. *Create* is the term we're familiar with, but I'll address that later. Rollo May, in his book *The Courage to Create*, says, "Creativity is a necessary sequel to being." I feel that if I don't get what's inside of me, outside of me, then I will not have lived my purpose. I believe that I have something to contribute, whether I'm worthy in someone else's eyes or not. If I don't share these things, I will feel, as May put it, that "[I] will have betrayed [my] community in failing to make [my] contribution to the whole." I know that God uses us for His purposes, and He fulfills us along the way.

There are so many worshipers, of many things, but my focus is God. If someone claims Christ, then he or she is a worshiper of Christ. So this book is for Christians, of all positions, experiences, and maturities. Find encouragement in the words and thoughts to come. I hope and pray that this collection brings great things to your gatherings. Remember that God stands with us, so let us have no fear as we fight.

> *"The place where God calls you is the place where your deep gladness and the world's deep hunger meet."*
> —*Frederick Buechner*

AS WE FIGHT:
A Weekly Guide Through the Warfare of Worship

The battles you face no longer await; they are here and now. As a worship leader, pastor, associate leader, volunteer, servant, or simply a church attender, we have all experienced worship as warfare, spiritually and sometimes physically, mentally, and emotionally. Whether you see yourself as a creative person or not, you will find yourself at the frontline of battle. And in the midst of such battles, there is limited time; valuable time that could be saved by having supplemental resources, proper tools and weapons, and a tested battle plan. So I wrote this book to provide a valuable resource to help refine your tools and plans.

As a tool meant to guide you, this book, filled with fifty-two devotionals, will alleviate some of the demands of your job or schedule and help you find fresh ways to inspire team members and stay inspired yourself, while staying relevant to the season at hand. With the year broken into four quarters, spanning three months each, the ideas stay relevant and fresh in this supplemental guide for worship leaders and worshipers alike. You'll find a timely encouragement for each week that often accompany the cultural norms of the season. There is a fifth week in each quarter to compensate for longer months and give extra insight when needed. In addition, I've included some Back Pocket Devos to keep handy.

Having led worship for nearly ten years and heading up worship over the entire student ministry across three campuses, I have used many of these devotionals and been met with much success. I've served in various churches, and more importantly, at various levels. I began leading worship in small groups. God has given me a passion for worship and anointings for different seasons. Through His guidance, I've learned so much about submitting to authority while maintaining the vigor for battle. I know what it's like to be the Private, who must blindly follow nearly every order. But as a good soldier, I have moved up in ranks according to God's timeline, and have had the privilege of serving as a leader, and now a leader of leaders. It has not been an easy journey. The battles are real, and they aren't just on the stage or supernatural.

What I had to fight to learn is now available to you in a well-organized and straight forward way. I've worked hard to take away the excuses you may have: not enough time to prepare an encouragement, not wanting to pull a watered down word out of your hat (I'm being nice, for now), not feeling equipped to share, thinking everyone is tired of you talking, not trusting your own words, or the plethora (yeah, I went there) of reasons that have crossed your mind before.

I've thought all of those excuses and said a few. My wife (husbands, you understand the power of her words) has said some of them to me on occasion as well. It doesn't mean she was right, or wrong. So I went to the One who knows me best, my story, and how I fit into His story. He would stir my heart and call me closer to him. As I led my team, I naturally began to find encouragements that I felt were compelling, honest, and relevant. This book is the result of those leadings.

After launching our third campus, a video teaching campus, I had the privilege to be the worship leader. I truly believe that God used the sparks from our devotional times as catalysts for His glory. God has moved and is moving, and I'm honored to be a part of it. We can only ever attribute any good to Him.

These are real quotes I've heard, as best I can remember: "People really worship here." "This campus's worship atmosphere is amazing." "It's so refreshing to be part of such an authentic service." "There is such a sweet yet powerful spirit of worship here."

We strive for excellence as another form of honoring Him, but there is always room to grow, and I know you feel the same about your own home church.

I promise to be honest, even painfully so at times. I promise that you will be challenged in the best possible ways through this study. As a leader, you will grow in your leadership and credibility among your team. As a team member or volunteer, you will grow in wisdom and truth. As we go on this journey together, God will make more things known to you than you could find on your own.

What You Will Get from This Book

What you have to look forward to (if you truly dive in):

- More free time through the week and during pre-service preparations

- Tried, tested, and trustworthy encouragements available when they are most needed

- Feeling better equipped to lead moments and meetings

- Relevant and time-sensitive connections to the real world in real time

- More awareness of cultural trends

- Well-organized information which can be easily found and applied

- Increased intimacy with Christ

- More excitement, trust, and buy-in from your team and leadership

- Deeper understanding of the calling placed on each person's life, in every role

- A larger return on investment, monetarily and temporally

Who Is This Book For?

- Christians: every Christ follower is a worshiper

- Worship leaders: every person on stage is a worship leader in some capacity

- The Curious: those who want to know more about the culture of worship towards the Christian God in the modern world and the struggles that go along with it

Why Is This For You?

- There never seems to be enough time, resources, focus, expectation, and/or motivation in the week leading up to the weekend services

- You're facing spiritual warfare, difficult relationships, divisiveness among team members or leadership, or uncertainties in your leadership or that of others

- There is no problem, and that's the problem! There is too much complacency

- A number of other reasons

Your Solution: aha, you thought I'd just hand it to you, but I'd rather just give you a hand! Keep reading for next steps!

You've already taken the best first step: recognizing that you can benefit from someone else's experiences. That's one wall of pride knocked down already!

And herein lies the warning! Your pride will tell you to tread carefully. Your own experiences will tell you that you've been right more often than wrong. You will place your calling above the wisdom and counsel of others who have been there before. These are just some of the battles you will face.

But you are already at war. You are already on the frontline. The power of this choice is no longer in your hands. Would you rather continue to stand alone, with the simple, primitive weapons you've forged on your own, allowing your pride to be the strongest weapon in your enemy's hands? Or would you stand with an army, with weapons forged throughout time by Christ Himself? I know what I have chosen. I hope you do this same.

> *"For the weapons of our warfare are not of the flesh but have divine power to destroy strongholds."*
> *—2 Corinthians 10:4*

What you do with this book will be a defining moment for you. Battles do come without warning, but more often they are expected, even planned. Your next battle awaits you, and the enemy's intent is this: to distract you from reading further. The battle is whether or not you will open this book once again. Don't leave it on the shelf or put it aside with the hope of reading it when there is time. No! You know the times of the battle already, those days leading up to the weekend service. Make your battle plan now: to have your next reading time scheduled. Just as you go to battle preparing for your task, your duty, use this book to supplement that training. Then, on the morning of the service, open it to that conveniently labeled week of the month, and confidently share it with your team, your leader, your congregation, or yourself once again.

In 2 Chronicles 32, the king of Assyria invaded Judah just after Hezekiah's acts of faithfulness in chapter 31. Hezekiah, the king of Judah, didn't rely on his own faithfulness, but instead began to *plan* and *act*. He built up walls and towers, made weapons and shields, set commanders, gathered the people, and encouraged them with this:

> *"Be strong and courageous. Do not be afraid or dismayed before the king of Assyria and all the horde that is with him, for there are more with us than with him. With him is an arm of flesh, but with us is the Lord our God, to help us and to fight our battles." And the people took confidence from the words of Hezekiah king of Judah."*
> *—2 Chronicles 32:5-8 (ESV)*

Worship is Warfare

Worship is a word that covers a lot of ground. When *worship* is mentioned from here on out, it is often in reference to the singing and musical portion of a church service. Sometimes, however, it means the entire service, as all of the elements (teaching, giving, praying, communion, baptism, etc.) are acts of worship. And just to throw you off, occasionally it means everything you do while breathing on this earth. As you can gather from this title heading, worship is warfare, in whichever capacity. *These battles are the collision of God's will, man's will, and the enemy's will, each one demanding worship in one way or another, while only One is truly worthy of it.*

In 2 Chronicles, Jehoshaphat feared men that were coming against him for battle. He sought the Lord and followed His command by doing what seemed insane. He sent the singers first into battle. God's ways are bigger than ours.

> "... he appointed those who were to sing to the Lord and praise him in holy attire, as they went before the army, and say, "Give thanks to the Lord for his steadfast love endures forever."
>
> "And when they began to sing and praise, the Lord set an ambush against the men of Ammon, Moab, and Mount Seir, who had come against Judah, so that they were routed. For the men of Ammon and Moab rose against the inhabitants of Mount Seir, devoting them to destruction, and when they had made an end of the inhabitants of Seir, they all helped to destroy one another."
> —2 Chronicles 20: 21-23

In this passage, we see that the singing of and to God *sent the enemy running!* It's amazing to see the way today's services are structured after this pattern of worship: praising God through song and music as the first charge of battle. God has powerful plans in music and worship towards Himself. He has shown us throughout time that He is capable of more than we can imagine. *What men may see as insanity is often what God uses to accomplish His goals.*

In the scriptures, we see this battle cry often: "Give thanks to the Lord, for His steadfast love endures forever." When we look to the enemy, other people, things of this earth, or even ourselves, we can easily lose hope. The tasks look more daunting, spirits are waning, the battle weighs heavily, and the enemy appears immovable. When we look to the Lord, however, we see victory already. We see that His burden is light because it is not something we carry alone. We have God Himself on our side. Or more correctly, we are on His side, the winning side.

> *"Do not be afraid and do not be dismayed at this great horde, for the battle is not yours but God's . . . You will not need to fight in this battle. Stand firm, hold your position, and see the salvation of the Lord on your behalf, O Judah and Jerusalem.' Do not be afraid and do not be dismayed. Tomorrow go out against them, and the Lord will be with you."*
> *—2 Chronicles 20:15, 17*

As you already know, there are multiple facets and seasons in battle. Here, the focus is on the fight against the enemy and supernatural forces; the fight against internal forces; and the fight of the external, specifically regarding relationships and people, from those in leadership all the way down to the occasional church attender.

Within each season, there are topics that reach outside of that season's fight. The truth is that all of these battles happen at various times and often simultaneously. So use this guide to help dig into your own services and theologies. This is by no means a comprehensive study, but rather a potent dose of perspective as you approach your weekly services.

You have authority from God Himself, and you are not alone; you are led by a mighty warrior, the God of the universe, whose name is Lord of lords, King of kings. No enemy can even stand against Him; they fall to their knees or fall like lightning (Luke 10:18). As you reflect on these thoughts, soak in the bits of His Word that are peppered throughout. Next, we'll dive into this statement: Worship is Life.

> *"The Lord is a man of war; the Lord is His name."*
> *—Exodus 15:3*

Worship is Life

> *"The most important aspect of Christianity is not the work we do, but the relationship we maintain and the surrounding influence and qualities produced by that relationship. That is all God asks us to give our attention to, and it is the one thing that is continually under attack."*
> *—Oswald Chambers,*
> *"My Utmost for His Highest" (8/4)*

This book isn't a foray into worship itself. It's meant to be a supplemental guide for weekly services. It will help show the value and weight that worship carries. Worship represents something so huge that it cannot fully be explained or understood. It is life itself. Worship is life.

> *"I appeal to you therefore, brothers, by the mercies of God, to present your bodies as a living sacrifice, holy and acceptable to God, which is your spiritual worship."*
> *—Romans 12:1*

- Our act of spiritual worship is to offer our bodies to God: our actions, thoughts, and all that we encompass.

- Everything we do in life is worship; worship, simply, is giving attention to one thing above all other things.

> *And whatever you do, in word or deed, do everything in the name of the Lord Jesus, giving thanks to God the Father through him."*
> *—Colossians 3:17*

- We must maintain focus and strive to be like Christ.

> *"And you, who once were alienated and hostile in mind, doing evil deeds, he has now reconciled in his body of flesh by his death, in order to present you holy and blameless and above reproach before him, if indeed you continue in the faith, stable and steadfast, not shifting from the hope of the gospel that you heard, which has been proclaimed in all creation under heaven, and of which I, Paul, became a minister."*
> *—Colossians 1:21-23*

- Therefore, i.e., ergo, henceforth, and so on: Worship is life! It is all that we do, every moment on earth with breath in our lungs is to be lived as worship to our God.

Life is full of battles. It's ultimately a war for the souls of man. The beautiful hope that we carry is due to the fact that the victory is sealed. Christ has overcome, God is the champion, and the Holy Spirit reigns in our hearts. However, it doesn't mean that every battle is done; it doesn't mean the fight mustn't occur.

Throughout this book, you'll grow in knowledge of four fights, one per quarter. You've been engaging in these warfares already, and bringing them to light will only make the battles more real, but also more manageable. You'll have more tools, better weapons, and strengthened fortitude to face each combatant:

- The fight against the enemy

- The fight against culture

- The fight against flesh

- The fight *with* leadership

Take these devotionals however you'd like. Read them to your team members or leaders every Sunday morning as you fight, or binge read it in its entirety. Either way, open your perspective enough to allow God to use it for His glory, however He may see fit to do so.

Your Thoughts

For your own study, ask yourself these questions each month:

- How is my team responding?

- Is the information relevant?

- What is something that wasn't mentioned but seemed especially pertinent for a specific day/week/month/season?

- Other things I've studied this month: _____

I'd love to hear from you! If you feel any of your answers could benefit others, please submit them at aswefightbook.com/contact. Thanks!

I. The Fight Against the Enemy

Before we dive into the devotionals, let's get to know our enemy. Going into battle with an unknown adversary is not wise, especially one of this magnitude.

> *"For we do not wrestle against flesh and blood, but against the rulers, against the authorities, against the cosmic powers over this present darkness, against the spiritual forces of evil in the heavenly places."*
> *—Ephesians 6:12*

> *"For though we walk in the flesh, we are not waging war according to the flesh. For the weapons of our warfare are not of the flesh but have divine power to destroy strongholds."*
> *—2 Corinthians 10:3-4*

The enemy has already lost. He staged a coup and was struck out of heaven like lightning. Like lightning, like the snap of our fingers, like a flash so instantaneous that we would miss it if we were not looking for it. We often imagine a third of the angels battling it out for some lengthy amount of time, but Christ said that he saw Satan fall instantly. That's our God! That's our Warrior King!

The enemy has already lost

> *"And he said to them, "I saw Satan fall like lightning from heaven. Behold, I have given you authority to tread on serpents and scorpions, and over all the power of the enemy, and nothing shall hurt you. Nevertheless, do not rejoice in this, that the spirits are subject to you, but rejoice that your names are written in heaven."*
> *—Luke 10:18-20*

Satan is defeated and will always be defeated. He is fighting a losing battle. A man who knows he is losing will do some crazy things: he will stop playing by any rules; he will have no honor; he will manipulate, cheat, throw a Hail Mary, and revert to desperation. The enemy wants us to be as miserable as he is. He wants to thwart God's plans. He wants to steal, kill, and destroy. He is an imitator of God, going around like a roaring lion while Christ is the lion of Judah, the One who has no equal and no need to devour for He does not starve.

> *"And one of the elders said to me, 'Weep no more; behold, the Lion of the tribe of Judah, the Root of David, has conquered, so that he can open the scroll and its seven seals.'"*
> *—Revelation 5:5*

> *"Humble yourselves, therefore, under the mighty hand of God so that at the proper time he may exalt you, casting all your anxieties on him, because he cares for you. Be sober-minded; be watchful. Your adversary the devil prowls around like a roaring lion, seeking someone to devour. Resist him, firm in your faith, knowing that the same kinds of suffering are being experienced by your brotherhood throughout the world. And after you have suffered a little while, the God of all grace, who has called you to his eternal glory in Christ, will himself restore, confirm, strengthen, and establish you. To him be the dominion forever and ever. Amen."*
> *—1 Peter 5:6-11*

Stand Firm

> *"Be sure to put your feet in the right place, then stand firm."*
> *—Abraham Lincoln*

In the battle, upon being struck, a warrior must plant his feet in order to hold his ground. However, if the soldier isn't aware of the terrain, he could possibly put his faith in the wrong footing, be it sand, mud, or a slippery slope. Maybe it looks firm, maybe some others have walked close to that very spot, maybe it looks just like a place the soldier has been before. But there is always the risk that something slick lies beneath.

You must go into battle ready, clothed, and aware of what's ahead, as much as possible. Don't go into a worship service without being spiritually protected and armed. Holding to your own convictions without aligning them to the Word of God is dangerous. You're putting your faith in a footing that isn't tested or true, even if it seems to be so.

> *"Do not have your concert first, and then tune your instrument afterwards. Begin the day with the Word of God and prayer, and get first of all into harmony with Him."*
> —Hudson Taylor

> *"Finally, be strong in the Lord and in the strength of his might. Put on the whole armor of God, that you may be able to stand against the schemes of the devil. For we do not wrestle against flesh and blood, but against the rulers, against the authorities, against the cosmic powers over this present darkness, against the spiritual forces of evil in the heavenly places. Therefore take up the whole armor of God, that you may be able to withstand in the evil day, and having done all, to stand firm. Stand therefore, having fastened on the belt of truth, and having put on the breastplate of righteousness, and, as shoes for your feet, having put on the readiness given by the gospel of peace. In all circumstances take up the shield of faith, with which you can extinguish all the flaming darts of the evil one; and take the helmet of salvation, and the sword of the Spirit, which is the word of God, praying at all times in the Spirit, with all prayer and supplication. To that end, keep alert with all perseverance, making supplication for all the saints, and also for me, that words may be given to me in opening my mouth boldly to proclaim the mystery of the gospel, for which I am an ambassador in chains, that I may declare it boldly, as I ought to speak."*
> —Ephesians 6:10-20

Now that we know more about the enemy and our fight against him, let's move into the first month of the year with confidence!

Rough Starts

January: ah, the month of newness. It's so refreshing to imagine starting over, clearing off the slate, a second (or more likely thirteenth) chance. *So fresh and so clean clean.* If you understand that reference, you're in good company, and you're reading the right book to help lead you (us) to repentance! If you don't recognize it, I applaud your holiness, or home-schooled background. (*Please acknowledge the pinch of chagrin I've thrown in to loosen things up.*)

However, while it's freeing to start fresh, not everything that is new is all good. There's usually a not-so-glamorous catch to the glimmering newness. I once joked with my brothers about writing a rap that included the misleading phrase "I'm as fresh as cow crap." Please excuse my language, I know "rap" can be a bad word to some people. You can't spell "crap" without it! #thatsajoke #dontfreakout

I digress, that *shouldn't* happen much from here on out . . . no promises though! My point is that even though the first month of each year brings so much "newness," not all of it will be beautiful. If you've had any children yet, you understand this extremely well. The little angelic cherub that smiles as he farts may bring music or joy to your heart. But there is often more to that fart than meets the ear. And the same is true for resolutions, fasts, church services, and all that we get so excited about in January.

Do not be afraid though. This year needs you, and all that newness needs taming; you are being equipped to handle it. Just reading this book helps to bring the necessary awareness for change. You are going to be a catalyst for life change by your leadership and by your trust in God.

The battle is fraught with danger. It is saturated with peril. But it also drips with hope. It begs to be squeezed, like a weighty sponge, with all that liquid middle, all that potential energy waiting to be expelled. Like bubble wrap, it just yearns to be popped. Like your friend's head-sized gum bubble when she non-verbally indicates that you definitely should not touch it. But we do it anyways. And we're going to hit this year running, regardless of what reservations we may have.

What other choice do we have? If you have ever experienced God, truly tasted His paradoxical goodness, then you must have more. His presence completely satisfies, but you still feel as if you need more. It's like ice cream but good for you. No, we don't have a choice any more. We are soldiers, enlisted in God's army, fighting for the advancement of His kingdom. It's time to step up to bigger and better weapons. Let us fight! Onward, soldiers!

What you have to look forward to this month:

- Finding identity in your leadership

- A different take on resolutions

- What the universe throws at you

- One of the many privileges you have

- Why the enemy fights dirty

Unashamed Worship

My wife makes fun of me for it, but I use this same encouragement in one particular song, nearly every time I lead it: "We are unashamed to proclaim the name of Jesus in this place." It just rolls right off the tongue, right? It pumps me up and the congregation as well. A powerful word or action helps to release those heavy weights hooked to everyone's wrists, those chains and shackles that won't let their arms go higher than a hand shake.

A common reservation you may have is to let the congregation or others determine your worship or fervor. You must keep in mind that from any position, you are a leader. You should never let the congregation lead you in energy or engagement. In moments of worship in song, *you are to lead, not to be led*, except by the guidance of the Holy Spirit of course.

Don't be ashamed of your worship. As a father watches his child dance for him, he does not judge, but rather delights in every whimsical and expressive movement. The same is true as you lead. *Don't hold back your joy, on the stage or in your life.*

An argument will be made for distraction. You may need to ease your congregation into it, but don't tarry too long. After encouraging each team member to lead with vigor, you may now have what seems to be the opposite problem. The most distracting person on the stage is the one *not moving*, or remaining *reserved*. Press forward with this word: *Do not be ashamed of your worship, for your Father is not ashamed of it. In fact, He lavishes in it.*

> Don't hold back your joy, on the stage or in your life.

> *"How great is the love the Father has lavished on us, that we should be called children of God! And that is what we are!"*
> *—1 John 3:1*

As silly as it may seem, if you feel the call to sing louder, become more expressive, and show more passion, then don't let anything stop you. Don't think, "How can this be an act of fighting?" It's not up to you to always understand how or why something can work. A good soldier doesn't question his orders, he just follows the command.

No Resolutions

I promised controversy; this may be the first one to rub you wrong. If so, *you're welcome*. My wife really dislikes when I somewhat jokingly say, "Conviction comes from the Holy Spirit."

New Years' resolutions are painful. They start with such hope and promise, but also with an inevitable doom that looms over them; this foreboding fog floats around as everyone chooses-their-own-adventure. You can pretty much put the top ten resolutions in a hat and draw one out, landing you right alongside everyone else.

My challenge to you is to not make a resolution this year. Or better yet, change your perspective of what that is. Walking in God's will is day to day, not January to March.

- Resolutions imply failure and disappointment; God's word implies hope that does not disappoint.

> *"Now hope does not disappoint, because the love of God has been poured out in our hearts by the Holy Spirit who was given to us."*
> *—Romans 5:5 (NKJV)*

- Resolutions require submission as the primary mode for life change; God's word requires gratitude and outward focus to live in His will.

> *"Rejoice always, pray without ceasing, give thanks in all circumstances; for this is the will of God in Christ Jesus for you."*
> *—1 Thessalonians 5:16-18*

- Resolutions rely on us; God's word changes us daily to be more like Him, the only truly reliable One.

Make a resolution to not make a resolution. I know, if you do that, then you've done what you said you wouldn't, and it tears a tiny hole in the fabric of the universe. But there is some power in that phrase and thought. Instead, do what you already know is right: read His word, worship Him for who He is and not just what He's done, communicate with Him, be grateful, find your friend again. In doing these things, let God change you for the better. And this will not leave you empty, exhausted, and defeated by March. No, quite the opposite. In Him, you find strength. In your weakness, His strength is made known, is made perfect.

> *"But he said to me, "My grace is sufficient for you, for my power is made perfect in weakness." Therefore I will boast all the more gladly of my weaknesses, so that the power of Christ may rest upon me. For the sake of Christ, then, I am content with weaknesses, insults, hardships, persecutions, and calamities. For when I am weak, then I am strong."*
> *—1 Corinthians 12:9-10*

Universe vs. God

When it feels like the universe is against you, remember that God is for you. He is always fighting for you. He formed the universe by speaking: uttering word, breath, and inspiration. He can take the universe, the breath that it was and do with it what He wishes. He holds it all in His mighty right hand.

> *"Our God is in the heavens; he does all that he pleases."*
> *—Psalms 115:3*

So when life brings you to your knees, let your life bring worship to the King. Let your breath be inspired by His. Let it be praise to His majesty. What beautiful knowledge it is that He loves you, not only because He is good, but because it pleases Him. It pleases Him to know you.

> *"For great is your love, reaching to the heavens; your faithfulness reaches to the skies."*
> *—Psalms 57:10*

> *"For as high as the heavens are above the earth, so great is his love for those who fear him."*
> *—Psalms 103:11*

Front Row Seats

> *"Tell me the facts and I'll learn. Tell me the truth and I'll believe. But tell me a story and it will live in my heart forever."*
> —An old Native American proverb

No matter where you sit or serve in the building, you all have front row seats to life change. If you are on stage, you can see the faces of worshipers calling out to God. It's an amazing thing to behold. If you are in the congregation, you can watch leaders at the front lines worshiping or look to your left and right to see your compadres singing the song God has given them.

It's in the knowing and the not knowing, the experienced and the unforeseen, the lived and missed, the promise and the pain, the healing and the hurt

You need to get to know the people around you, to know their stories. When you do, you find more courage than ever while leading, singing, or serving. As a worship leader, I get to see people engaging and experiencing not just heart-felt, but *soul*-felt worship. When I know their stories, what they've gone through or are going through, it leads me to brokenness and bravery; from introspection to inspiration, it perfects my perspective. I see people who have cancer and terminal illnesses, who have lost children in miscarriages or otherwise, who are in the midst of divorce, and who are struggling with addictions that hold stronger than any man-made chain. I also see people who have been blessed beyond measure worshiping alongside those who stand in want. I see people praising in the good and the bad, trusting in a God that operates outside of our rules.

I've seen my mother, who has battled the most aggressive form of brain cancer for over 18 months so far. I've seen her stretching her hands to the Father, even the hand that is affected from partial paralysis, caused by tumors pressing against her brain. God gave me that picture, a reminder, of what she will be doing for eternity, regardless of how long she has with us in this life.

It's in the knowing and the not knowing, the experienced and the unforeseen, the lived and missed, the promise and the pain, the healing and the hurt. And you won't get to that depth of worship without knowing those who know God, to experience Him in ways deeper than most of us can imagine.

> *"Now to him who is able to do far more abundantly than all that we ask or think, according to the power at work within us, to him be glory in the church and in Christ Jesus throughout all generations, forever and ever. Amen."*
> *—Ephesians 3:20-21*

> *"Therefore God has highly exalted him and bestowed on him the name that is above every name, so that at the name of Jesus every knee should bow, in heaven and on earth and under the earth, and every tongue confess that Jesus Christ is Lord, to the glory of God the Father."*
> *—Philippians 2:9-10*

Unfair Fight

Yes, the enemy fights dirty. He doesn't play by the same rules that we do. He can even step outside of many of our rules, and has an army of his own. No, the fight isn't fair. People don't even play by the rules. Some are sneaky and manipulative. Some are just plain ignorant of what should and shouldn't be said or done. No, the fight isn't fair. And there's the flesh, the sinful nature of man that fights against us from the inside. We are attacked on every front, every side, inwards and out. The fight isn't fair. But let me tell you why the fight isn't fair.

The fight isn't fair because we have our God

The fight isn't fair because we have our God. The fight isn't fair to the enemy because he has already been defeated. No, the fight isn't fair. It isn't fair to people who want us to fail because of the multitude of promises we have in His word.

> *"For I know the plans I have for you, declares the Lord, plans for welfare and not for evil, to give you a future and a hope. Then you will call upon me and come and pray to me, and I will hear you. You will seek me and find me, when you seek me with all your heart. I will be found by you, declares the Lord, and I will restore your fortunes and gather you from all the nations and all the places where I have driven you, declares the Lord, and I will bring you back to the place from which I sent you into exile."*
> *—Jeremiah 29:11-14*

No, the fight isn't fair. It isn't fair to the flesh, the natural, that has to battle the God-powered spirit and the supernatural. We are no longer slave to fear and sin. So whenever you think, "This isn't fair," you're right! Satan will fight dirty, attacking us in ways we can't handle alone. But we do not fight alone. We fight alongside our great God, against whom Satan is no match. *None is greater than our God, none compare, none contend, none can stand face to face with His holiness and simply walk away.*

None is greater than our God, none compare, none contend

> *"No, in all these things we are more than conquerors through him who loved us. For I am sure that neither death nor life, nor angels nor rulers, nor things present nor things to come, nor powers, nor height nor depth, nor anything else in all creation, will be able to separate us from the love of God in Christ Jesus our Lord."*
> *—Romans 8:37-39*

Just Lovely

Love is patient. Love is kind . . . you know the rest; if not, check out 1 Corinthians 13. Love is wonderful, yet we choose to officially glorify love only one day per year. As with resolutions, danger lies within such dedicated, annual worship. Just as we are new each day, by God's grace and guidance, we should also celebrate love daily. And to better know, experience, and share love, we must go to its source.

> *"Anyone who does not love does not know God, because God is love."*
> *—1 John 4:8*

Love is a form of worship, worship is warfare; therefore, by the transitive property, love is war. *It is a bold act of war to live contradictory to the world.* The enemy thrives on despair, discontentment, disgust, miscommunication, and indifference. When we act in opposition to those things, i.e. in love, he writhes and loathes our existence, and fights back. So be prepared as we enter a season that celebrates the temporal high of what the world calls *love*, and combat it with true selfless love. Put on your armor and use love as a weapon of mass construction, carry Him to the world and fear not, for He is with you always.

> It is a bold act of war to live contradictory to the world.

> *"fear not, for I am with you;*
> *be not dismayed, for I am your God;*
> *I will strengthen you, I will help you,*
> *I will uphold you with my righteous right hand."*
> *—Isaiah 41:10*

What you have to look forward to this month:

- What you are made for

- Significance of your work

- Service as sacrifice

Worship Training

As I write, I am in the throes of sleep training our first child. It's exceptionally challenging to think and write while hearing that finely tuned frequency in his scream that I'm convinced is custom matched to my (and my wife's) inner ears. You know, the one that tingles your spine. And that's from a distance. When it's directly next to your face, I'm unable to hear pitches for a few minutes, due to the ringing and temporary hearing loss (hopefully not permanent, please don't let this be permanent).

We, and our congregations, go through similar trials as we grow in worship. Worship training is a lot like sleep training; it may be painful or awkward, and you don't know if it's even gonna work. *But you press on because whatever is on the other side is better than the alternative: to stay where we are.* If I let my son live a life of comfort forever, he would never grow to be the world-changer I hope for him to be. He would never experience most of the plans I may have for him. He would become a spoiled brat whose default setting is complaint.

But you press on because whatever is on the other side is better than the alternative: to stay where we are

As extreme as that sounds, there is even worse danger for standing still. As a matter of fact, there is no middle ground for a worshiper, for a Christ follower. At every moment, you are either moving closer to Him or further away. So challenge yourself and the congregation today in some act of worship, whether by the raising of hands or simply the obvious, but all-to-often avoided, act prompted by the phrase "Sing with us!"

They will sing frequencies, pitches, and notes that would never fit what we may traditionally call "music." But to God, to the Father, every note a child sings to Him is beautiful music. He is tuned into a frequency of our souls, one that surpasses human understanding of music, sound, and connection. One that communicates more than sound ever could. It's the awareness of brokenness coming into reconciliation with the recognition of the sovereignty of God. It's the collision of fear and trust, uncertainty and hope, weakness and faith, anguish and peace, hate and love. It's all of that and more. *Worship is what we are truly made for.*

Worship is what we are truly made for

Kingdom Significance

> *"For God will break the chains that bind his people."*
> —*Isaiah 9:4 (TLB)*

Your voice does not just operate in the physical world when you sing praises to God. It breaks chains. There are many references in the Psalms about this as well as New Testament accounts. Chains, iron gates, shackles, bonds, and the like symbolize restrictions and inflictions on our lives, whether it's due to addiction, circumstance, socio-economic status, physical or mental limitations, illness or disease, pride or arrogance, spiritual issues, and so much more. Through time of worship to Him, you lay down what you're unable to escape, and you allow Him to give you freedom. *It is not always what you expect, but it's always what you need.*

A lot of the weight you carry coincides with the bonds on your life, especially in the realm of disobedience. I often challenge people to lift their hands over their heads as a sign of obedience, and ultimately surrender, reminding them that there is freedom in even such a simple act as this. It's hard to lift your hands up when they're weighed down with so much doubt. But God will give you the strength if you just trust Him to. He will break those chains holding your hands to the ground. He will remove the gates that keep you behind His will for your life. He will use your single act of obedience to show you freedom you never knew that *you* could have.

A soul can be set free in worship.

That takes you and your people one step closer to God. There is an unknown amount of power in worship that transcends the finite mind. Any thing that ascribes glory to God has the potential to change a life for good. *A soul can be set free in worship,* therefore adding to the Kingdom of God. A person can experience more of Him which will allow others to experience more of God through that person. It's truly unlimited. There is kingdom significance to everything that you do. The world cannot encounter God without being affected.

"When we worship God as we ought that's when the nations listen."
—Edmund Clowney

Sacrifice of Praise

"God, we bring this sacrifice of praise to You, knowing that it doesn't compare to the sacrifice of Your Son. We bring this in honor of You. As we worship you today, thank you for that reminder of our unfair deal: that we get more than we give, having gained more than we gave."

Everything you do to prepare for a weekend service, from practicing instruments or song to praying and growing in expectation, are acts of worship themselves. These are small sacrifices of time, of praise, that you give to honor God with your best. They are your offerings, and you do them as you remember the incomparable sacrifice of Christ on the cross.

Sacrifice is a beautiful picture of love and obedience

When you consider your service as sacrifice, it may seem like an inconvenience, but it's actually an acknowledgement and reminder that you do this to honor Him. It also relieves the pressure of the performance aspect, re-aligns your purpose as a worshiper, and reminds you that His grace covers your shortcomings. Don't let the thought of sacrifice be a negative one. *Sacrifice is a beautiful picture of love and obedience.*

"Through him then let us continually offer up a sacrifice of praise to God, that is, the fruit of lips that acknowledge his name. Do not neglect to do good and to share what you have, for such sacrifices are pleasing to God."
—Hebrews 13:15-16

Made for This

Are we doing it right? Worship. I wonder this often, too often I'm afraid. I believe that we have a lot to learn and a long ways to go. For now though, we must work to reconcile our hoped-for forecast with the present climate. Sometimes worship leading, or even worshiping from any position on stage or off, feels like performing. There is certainly a performance nature to this modern worship style with the stage, lights, focus on excellence, showcasing talent, and other such factors. It's something we all wrestle with at times when we study the nature of a humble Christ follower. However, we are in this place at this time for a specific reason, and it's a simple one: to communicate.

As we sing, we are communicating, just like talking, but with more emphasis, more passion. Rather than performing a song, seek to communicate the message. It's about the story of God and the glory of God. When we perform, we are often passionate about ourselves, our talent, or the glory we receive. When we communicate, we are passionate about the message and the life change that comes out of it. And when the message is Christ, a living, transforming power, then we have the most reason for passionate delivery. In our passion, we can strive for excellence because excellence increases the potential for the message being received and utilized.

As we sing, we are communicating

So are we doing it right? That may not be up to us to discover at the present time, however:

- Keep studying and growing in wisdom and truth

- Stay curious, don't settle like some dense substance in a glass of liquid: when one part separates and sits at the bottom, it no longer affects the rest of the container

- Be hungry for truth: not yours or someone else's but God's

- Use your *rear-view mirror* sparingly, stay focused on what's directly in front of you and what's visible ahead, and glance at the mirror occasionally; don't fix your eyes on the past or you'll surely crash

> *"You have been called to something much greater. You have been redeemed by Jesus and adopted into His family, then called to lead His church. You have been given the gift of musical art to tell the gospel and connect people's hearts to their Savior. You have been made a teacher to mold people's thinking about who God is and what He has done."*
> —Stephen Miller,
> *Worship Leaders, We Are Not Rock Stars*

Spring's Super Bowl

Easter is fast approaching; the Super Bowl of church culture! It is a momentous celebration, but again, the remembrance of Christ's death and sacrifice are not to be 'saved' for that yearly jubilation. Just as we are new creations daily, who should experience and express love daily, we should also be in holy recollection of that perfect sacrifice at least weekly, if not daily. Fortunately, there are many amazing churches that meet weekly to be reminded of Christ. Without some consistent, if not daily, remembrance of Christ, there will be decay. It is life to know Him. Jesus calls Himself "the life" (John 14:6) and Colossians 3:4 says, "Christ, who is your life." *So any separation from Him is separation from life.* His word is likened to bread, or sometimes milk or meat; some combination of these is required daily for sustenance.

Any separation from Him is separation from life

If you are not walking towards Him, breathing in His grace, then you are walking away from Him. There is no standing still. Just like food, you either eat consistently or you starve. Just like breathing, you are either taking it in or sending it out. The in-betweens cannot last long enough to sustain you. To live apart from Him for any amount of time will lead to decay.

So let us do as the month calls for: March! Onward towards Christ, onwards with Him into battle; do so without hesitation, and have firm confidence in our God.

> *"Memory annihilates distance and over leapeth time, and can behold the Lord, though he be exalted in glory."*
> *—Charles Spurgeon*

What you have to look forward to this month:

- Facing your shelf life

- The fortune of failure

- What it means to ascribe

- Objective perspectives on those *rare* mess-ups

Fulfillment

Oh what a joy it is to serve God in such capacities as we do. Occasionally though it feels difficult, costly, or exhausting. When your attitude turn inward, you need to get outside of yourself. When you see ministry as madness, you need to be reminded of the powerful privileges you have in Christ.

As a servant on stage or off, God has ordained and anointed you for this specific time, for reasons of His own, and to fulfill the calling on your life. Find fulfillment by this: *as an offering of worship, give back to Him what He has given to you.* As a musician or production person, you get to use gifts that are from God Himself. Don't ever forget where they came from in the first place.

As an offering of worship, give back to Him what He has given to you

Sure, you may have played in garage bands or even stadium gigs where you fine-tuned your craft. Or perhaps you were a bedroom noodler who just couldn't get enough of it. Either way, the thing that drove you was passion, and sometimes talent. But both passion and talent first come from God. They are gifts. And never underestimate the gift of passion; *with God-given passion, no obstacle is too great.* (there's more of this in Week 3)

Additionally, and unfortunately, stage ministry has a shelf life; one day, you will be replaced. But what is happening at the core should have no dependence on that. You were made to worship. It's that simple. Regardless of what position you are in, you were first made to be a worshiper. Your heart cries out for the missing piece inside, the living

God. If you only find fulfillment on the stage, then you have missed the point entirely. *You must experience God off stage to be most effective on stage.*

> *"that you may know what is the hope to which he has called you, what are the riches of his glorious inheritance in the saints, and what is the immeasurable greatness of his power toward us who believe, according to the working of his great might."*
> *—Ephesians 1:18b-19*

Other than sharing valuable passages from above, dedicate 3-8 minutes of prayer and focus to God before your next service, and challenge your team to do the same.

Even If We Crash and Burn

> *"Just because something doesn't do what you planned it to do doesn't mean it's useless."*
> — *Thomas Edison*

There have been times when things have gone wrong, once or twice! Once, when one of my guitar strings broke (no, it wasn't the G-string *this* time), God gave me these words to share with the congregation, "Worship isn't about the music and instruments anyways; let's continue to sing and make Him known." Another time, I messed up the verses during the debut of a new song so I stopped and said, "Let's try this again; I really want you to get these words." Then I jumped back in at the next insertable moment. Make sure to have your Music Director or band ready for such improvised leadership calls.

No matter how much work is put into an event, sometimes things go wrong, at least according to your discerning, performance-based eyes. There are always possibilities, or more likely weekly realities, of technical difficulties, missed notes, forgotten lyrics, distracted leadership, and more. *When you worship, the enemy doesn't want you to succeed.*

When you worship, the enemy doesn't want you to succeed

Oh how beautiful it is that 'success' is different in God's eyes. Sometimes you do crash and burn. Sometimes the service goes sideways. Sometimes what seems like an anointed moment gets ripped away by a poorly planned transition or mishap. Occasionally, you walk away from a service with head hung low because something went 'wrong'.

Consider this: what if it's in God's plan for your service to tank? What if God meant to bring good from disaster? What if God is bigger than our service flow?

Sometimes you will fail, according to your rules. But God is bigger! You don't know what His plan is, but trust that it is good, just as He is good. Maybe that mistake humanizes you to someone in the congregation, and he or she learns a little more about grace or mercy. Maybe something your team thought was a great idea had terrible repercussions, so God allowed you to catch it early. Perhaps a team member is dealing with pride (who isn't?) and needed the humility. It's possible that you will never know why most things happen—good or bad—but it's all in God's hands, and He does what is good because He is good. Consider this prayer as a guide:

"Even if we crash and burn, if that's Your will, let it be so. For we know that You know better than us. If our shortcomings or failures will lift You up, let it be so. Help us to strive for excellence, and give us grace for when we fall short. Give us the words and actions to navigate those moments with humility and honor towards You."

"For my thoughts are not your thoughts,
neither are your ways my ways, declares the Lord.
For as the heavens are higher than the earth,
so are my ways higher than your ways
and my thoughts than your thoughts."
—Isaiah 55:8-9

"Have you not known? Have you not heard? The Lord is the
everlasting God, the Creator of the ends of the earth. He does not
faint or grow weary; his understanding is unsearchable."
—Isaiah 40:28

Gift-Bringer

It's easy to worship God for what He's done, especially when you recognize that your talents and passions are gifts from Him. Nearly everyone will praise a gift-bringer. Sometimes you bring your gifts back to Him *because* He gave them to you, even though He deserves praise regardless of what He's done. In doing so, you belittle who He is; you belittle what you claim as worship. *You must first worship God simply for who He is.*

You must first worship God simply for who He is

God is deserving of praise regardless of all that He's done. The Breather of the universe, majestic in splendor, the One who always has been and always will be, the infinite, the holy, the Almighty!

Wonderfully, He *is* good and has done great things. He has brought you gifts, from talent and passion to strength and peace. Now *you* can become the gift-bringer. Make an attempt to remember all that He has given you and attribute them to God as you worship. Ascribe to the Lord.

> *"Ascribe to the Lord, O heavenly beings, ascribe to the Lord glory and strength. Ascribe to the Lord the glory due his name; worship the Lord in the splendor of holiness."*
> *—Psalms 29:1-2*

Worship Ourselves

Sometimes you mess up. Occasionally it's a simple fumble that you can recover. But every so often, it's a complete turn-over, off-sides, penalties, flags flying, and plays brought to absolute halts. Fortunately, God has a sense of humor, and He shares it with you, sometimes with your willingness and sometimes without.

I don't know what this says about me, but I often find encouragement when others fail (this is not a good thing, but it is quite human). This is specifically so when it pertains to what I do, or where I have failed as well. If you're like me, then here is some of that 'encouragement' based on things I *may or may not* have said or done:

- "God, as we lead others in worship, help us to worship ourselves." Okay, so you know what I meant, but that is some improper syntax.

- "I'm gonna need some unashamed worship tonight!" I really hope I didn't get it.

- Start singing with the keyboard player . . . you don't realize they are in the wrong key . . . until the band comes in with the right key. Oh the pain of that moment! I used to not wish that on anyone. But I actually do now, I wish it on every worship leader at least once. The amount of laughter that it will bring everyone the rest of the day or year is worth it.

- Similar mishap: the band starts in the right key . . . you strum your first big chord and realize you've forgotten to move the capo! What a wonderful sound it is! Just do the quick, 'what went wrong?' head motion, or better yet, act like nothing is wrong and slyly change the capo position. Then strum with *nearly* the same confidence as the first time!

- Rambling encouragements . . . you get into a flow and then you say some weird alien phrase that completely knocks you, and everyone else, off track . . . yes, we get it, just move on with the set, and maybe rehearse a bit next time.

I'm sure you could add to this list quite easily. Make sure that you take such mistakes lightly. Remember, they are mistakes. We don't purposefully want things to fail. *The only failure in the mess-up is not handling it with grace.* WWJD, right? Well, first off, He wouldn't mess up!

"We all stumble in many ways. Anyone who is never at fault in what they say is perfect, able to keep their whole body in check."
—James 3:2

"If we say that we do not have any sin, we are deceiving ourselves and we're not being truthful to ourselves."
—1 John 1:8

"The Lord is compassionate and merciful, slow to get angry and filled with unfailing love. He will not constantly accuse us, nor remain angry forever. He does not punish us for all our sins; he does not deal harshly with us, as we deserve. For his unfailing love toward those who fear him is as great as the height of the heavens above the earth."
—Psalms 103:8-11

II. The Fight Against Culture

> *"Worship is no longer worship when it reflects the culture around us more than the Christ within us."*
> —A. W. Tozer

Chances are your church isn't a massive arena, people aren't waiting in line for the first song; heck, many barely make it in time for the message! It's easy to get frustrated with the culture. It's easy to call people out for being late when you're there two hours early. It's easy to give in or give up. It's easy to say "forget it!" and do your own thing. Sure, lots of those reactions are *easy*. Is that the life you're called to? One that is *easy*? I know His yoke is easy (Matthew 11:30, another lesson for another time), but many people in the Bible, and countless others since it's writing, speak of the difficulty of the Christian life. There are battles upon battles, and many are against culture, the society of the time. It is in these challenges that you must lean on God's power through your insufficiencies of understanding and direction.

> *"All our difficulties are only platforms for the manifestations of His grace, power and love."*
> —Hudson Taylor

The Power of Expectation

Ah, the after-Easter breather, the old birds chirping, bugle blowing at sunrise, wide stretching, lazy, no-work-this-Monday feeling. For at least one day, it's okay to roll back over and hit snooze, guilt-free. "You've earned it," some distant voice whispers, in a tone that sounds oddly similar to your own. Those are some of the great moments of this life. Winter has packed up the cold and moved on for now, and spring is coming into full bloom.

If your church is like many others, this so-called "slow" season isn't very slow at all. We like to believe that it is, and maybe that ignorance or placebo is what it takes to keep moving forward.

Either way, there is an air of shoulder slumping relaxation throughout spring and as summer comes along. Enjoy it, but make the best use of it that you can.

You know that the job never really ends, but occasionally there is grace that allows you to re-focus and get your head on straight again. During these rare gifts, make sure to focus on the health of your team and your processes. The products, services, and volunteer engagement may be excellent, but there is always room to perfect each process. These are great times to get back to the core of what called you to lead people in the first place: a passion to see them grow in knowledge and wisdom of worship towards God. You have deep stirrings, such as discipleship of team members, spiritual depth studies, songwriting, and more. However, while hope runs on good intentions, it's constant planning and consistent execution that move dreams to reality.

One thing to be wary of is the tendency to lower your expectations during this season. You'll hear people expecting lower numbers and smaller turnouts to events due to the nice weather, higher travel rate, or just a lower overall sense of spiritual importance. It does make sense: numbers suffer at churches during spring and summer months, perhaps having to do with the better weather or more likely the ever-changing schedules due to traveling and such. Also, some people do not feel the inward pull to attend church as there is an overall increase in happiness when the sun is out, especially compared to the doom and gloom of transitioning seasons; fall and winter are more often when people turn inward and recognize their deep need for something greater than themselves. While this is evident in society, the world's culture shouldn't drive the church's culture. It's quite the opposite actually. The church is meant to be the catalyst for change in society, counter-cultural, challenging to social norms.

"You are the salt of the earth, but if salt has lost its taste, how shall its saltiness be restored? It is no longer good for anything except to be thrown out and trampled under people's feet. You are the light of the world. A city set on a hill cannot be hidden. Nor do people light a lamp and put it under a basket, but on a stand, and it gives light to all in the house. In the same way, let your light shine before others, so that they may see your good works and give glory to your Father who is in heaven."
—Matthew 5:13-16

During my second year leading the worship ministry for our student services, I heard leaders falling into the culture trap of low expectations. I, being the rebel that I'm told I am, refused to accept that. I challenged us to expect more than that. Throughout that summer, we actually experienced *growth* in numbers and engagement. That's right, not just breaking even but growth! Of course, that was God's doing, but I do think that our attitudes of expectation made a huge difference in our service planning and execution as well as the morale of volunteers and attenders alike.

The summer is an amazing opportunity to grow in depth even if you don't grow any wider. Be expectant. Be energized. Be the challenge to the culture, not for the sake of advancing your agenda but to advance His kingdom, to go headlong into battle without fear, to carry that bright light into the unknown darkness knowing that God is on your side when you are on His! And continue to dig into His word for guidance, wisdom, and courage.

Ten or Ten Thousand

Lead the same, whether it's for ten or ten thousand. God is worthy of our praise regardless, and sometimes it needs to just be His child dancing and singing for Him directly. Energy from the congregation definitely helps; enjoy that when it comes, but know that not everyone worships the same. Everyone is on their own journey of understanding worship and how they should participate in it. Also, many worship centers are following a trend today of being smaller and more intimate. Of course, stadium churches are massively popular, but there's something about doing life together with people you actually know and grow with. Everyone yearns for connection to another person, whether they're cognizant of it or not. There is little room for fostering relationships at a stadium event; however, it's natural to connect to people relationally in a room where each person can see every face.

Lead the same, whether it's for ten or ten thousand

If you are recording services to be broadcast, then your energy and leadership usually needs to be over-exaggerated. Everything on camera looks smaller than it feels. Often that's also true for anything you do on stage. When you think you nearly jumped off the stage in vigorous passion, most people saw a small hop. You think you're burning a circle with a five foot radius in your area, but you've only moved six inches to either side. To exaggerate an action may feel fake, I understand that. It's something you grow into as it becomes more authentic with time. I don't often recommend the old *fake it til you make it* motto, but it loosely applies here. You have to step out in faith, figuratively and literally. Seek the scriptures about dancing before the Lord, as well as other physical expressions of worship. *You can find a list of these in the "7 Strategies to Strengthen Your Worship" if you subscribe at aswefightbook.com.*

Learn more about leading, inspiring, and encouraging people to join in on the celebration. Remember that God is worthy of all you can bring Him and deserves your unashamed praise! If you still can't reconcile this, then focus on Him. *It is your duty in His army to fight on His behalf and not your own.* Let the worries of this world melt away as you celebrate the Savior!

> *"Praise the LORD!*
> *Sing to the LORD a new song,*
> *his praise in the assembly of the godly!*
> *Let Israel be glad in his Maker;*
> *let the children of Zion rejoice in their King!*
> *Let them praise His name with dancing,*
> *making melody to Him with tambourine and lyre!*
> *For the LORD takes pleasure in His people;*
> *He adorns the humble with salvation.*
> *Let the godly exult in glory;*
> *let them sing for joy on their beds.*
> *Let the high praises of God be in their throats*
> *and two-edged swords in their hands,*
> *to execute vengeance on the nations*
> *and punishments on the peoples,*
> *to bind their kings with chains*
> *and their nobles with fetters of iron,*
> *to execute on them the judgment written!*
> *This is honor for all his godly ones.*
> *Praise the LORD!"*
> *—Psalms 149*

Christ or Bust

Society is moving towards a much more polarizing culture when it comes to religion, true religion: Christianity or none, the truth or not the truth, the living God or all the other gods, Christ or bust. Currently, the lines are skewed, blurred by political correctness and universal morality. The days of calling oneself a Christian and backing it up are coming. One who identifies with Christ will have to make very public decisions on the matter. This matters in the warfare of worship for several reasons, one of which is the stage.

We are in a performance based culture via American Idol, The Voice, America's Got Talent, etc. We glorify the stage and the person; this alone discredits the true Source by ignoring Him altogether. We want others to live the life we want as we want to live the lives that others do. It's all mixed up and our recognition of God is lost in it. To affect the culture, we must seek righteousness, that is Christ and His plan for our lives, whether it's as a humble worship leader or a humble recording artist. We must fight against the culture to redeem the platforms that God has provided for us to share His messages of hope, joy, love, peace, and more, which all culminate to Christ.

> We shouldn't treat the church stage as a place of performance, but rather a place of communicating the gospel of Christ

How do we do this? One of the ways is by not giving in to the culture. *We shouldn't treat the church stage as a place of performance but rather a place of communicating the gospel of Christ.* We're to run to God first for guidance in every situation, seeking every opportunity to share His love. And we must love. Above all, love. Yes, sometimes we have to "take one for the team" as they say. Other times we should "stand up for what we believe in." Isn't in funny how you can use quotes to prove almost any point?

> *"I pray that you will understand the words of Jesus, 'Love one another as I have loved you.' Ask yourself, 'How has he loved me? Do I really love others in the same way?' Unless this love is among us, we can kill ourselves with work and it will only be work, not love. Work without love is slavery."*
> —*Mother Teresa*

- Pray for people, not positions: those who seek to be exalted and get it are missing greater rewards in Heaven, for theirs is only of this earth. (see Matthew 6)

- See others as image bearers of God: if you see God in and at work in them, your perspective will change. (Genesis 1:27)

- Serve and lead to the potential of the people: expect greatness from every person, let their mishaps be what surprise you. (see Proverbs 11:23-25)

- True greatness in the Kingdom of Heaven is serving others: Christ came to serve, let us follow that perfect example. (see Matthew 20:28, Mark 10:45, John 13:1-17)

- Lay down your life for others: set aside your desires, even your needs at times, for the betterment of someone else's growth in God. (see John 15:13)

> *"A new commandment I give to you, that you love one another: just as I have loved you, you also are to love one another. By this all people will know that you are my disciples, if you have love for one another."*
> —*John 13:34*

Don't Run with Scissors

I love a good, clean prank, especially in literature. One of my favorites is one by Benjamin Franklin. He wrote to a scientific academy, asking them to find a drug that could control the smell of one's gaseous expulsions, or discharging of wind. He put it more frankly when he said such discovery would be worth a "fart-hing." I read about it, appropriately enough, in the book *Fart Proudly*. Obviously, people would flock to such a drug; I know I would, if not for my wife's sake. People chase lies; they want to find and hear things that agree with them, such as that quick-fix pill for an unfixable problem. Then they get upset when they find truth instead.

The Bible is likened to a two-edged sword. It cuts precisely, and it cuts deep, to the marrow actually. Have you ever been cut that way? Physically? It's got to hurt! What would your reaction be? I know what I'd do. Actually, I had a similar experience. I lost my eye when I was eleven years old. I was hit with a lawn dart. Yes, I'm a statistic now. What would you imagine my first reaction to be? Not the smartest thing, but I ripped it out immediately. There was something foreign in me that wasn't supposed to be there! Did I mention that I was eleven. It was pretty intense.

When someone is confronted with the Word of God, it can feel foreign. I guarantee it can hurt. Cutting to the marrow, to the deepest part of an issue, usually does. Everyone knows not to run with scissors. So be careful with the Bible. Don't run with it. Carry it with care.

If you haven't caught up yet, it's April, fools! As far as everything above, I'll let you decipher fact from fiction.

What you have to look forward to this month:

- Peace in imperfection

- Some clever word play

- The Shelby Cobra!

- A lesson in waiting

- One mystery of newness

He Perfects Our Offerings

Look ahead; the stage is set, the battle awaits next month as it did last month. And it will continue. Battle after battle, fight after fight. And with God's guidance, victory after victory. Very few battles are won in spontaneity. Most often, they are well planned and precisely executed. The beauty is that we have something bigger on our side, and that is grace. God himself, in His glorious grace, His matchless ways, sent His son to be the perfect offering.

Now, because of that, Christ perfects our offerings. Whatever we bring to God is covered by the perfect blood of Christ because God is deserving of only that. His nature is pure, and He can only be approached that way. *Christ is that avenue, that connection from our depravity and weakness to God's goodness and holiness.*

Christ is that avenue, that connection from our depravity and weakness to God's goodness and holiness

Rest in the fact that whatever happens is part of His plan. If the service falls apart, God will still be exalted. Do we ever stop to consider that mistakes allow people to experience God the most? The reason testimonies are attractive is because they are riddled with wrong decisions, just like every person's life. The power comes from recognizing a perfect God in the midst of our imperfections, in the midst of our great need for One who can live up to His promises.

We have all fallen short, and we've all experienced broken promises, even if it's a simple mistake on the stage, with lyrics or in a transition. When we trust that God is ultimately in control, those details that we've magnified in our perspectives will find their proper context. Everything plays into God's amazing story. Even the mistakes . . . especially the mistakes.

> *"For by a single offering he has perfected for all time those who are being sanctified."*
> *—Hebrews 10:14*

You Get What You PRAY For

Ooh, how catchy is that?! If the pastor said that, I guarantee you'd hear some gasps of approval as well as the scrambling of paper and pens across the congregation. I've noticed such turns of phrase take an entire room captive, mostly older women. Don't judge though, there is some powerful truth in these words.

God isn't some child who holds what is His in clenched fists with a scowl that says, "No one else can have this, it's MINE!" He is one who wants good for His children. The Bible is filled with promises through prayer.

> *"Ask, and it will be given to you; seek, and you will find; knock, and it will be opened to you. For everyone who asks receives, and the one who seeks finds, and to the one who knocks it will be opened."*
> *—Matthew 7:7-8*

For your prayers to be most effective, you must strive to be holy. Work towards righteousness, which is not a thing, but rather the person of Christ. *Righteousness cannot be had, but it is someone who can be known.* You can't find the results of righteousness by simply looking for them. They are by-products of chasing Christ. (Conrad, *Holidazed*)

"Blessed are those who hunger and thirst for righteousness, for they shall be satisfied."
—*Matthew 5:6 (NASB)*

"The prayer of a righteous person has great power as it is working."
—*James 5:16*

"Truly, I say to you, whoever says to this mountain, 'Be taken up and thrown into the sea,' and does not doubt in his heart, but believes that what he says will come to pass, it will be done for him. Therefore I tell you, whatever you ask in prayer, believe that you have received it, and it will be yours."
—*Mark 11:23-24*

How can a mountain be taken up and thrown into the sea? Consider erosion. The wind slowly blowing the mountain apart, taking it up dust speck by dust speck, and carrying it into the sea. God is bigger than your mere mortal mind can comprehend. Ask today, and see what He does. *Expect a miracle and then let Him show it to you in a way that only He can.*

Expect a miracle and then let Him show it to you in a way that only He can

Open Hands Allow God's Plans

I remember one of the first times I tried to steal something. I also lied in the process. Isn't it funny how sin compounds upon itself? Trying to fix sin with sin is a losing battle; it's like digging a hole to get out of one.

I visited a family friend and got to play with his Hot Wheels cars. That's when it hit me: envy, one of the original sins. I saw that most amazing car, and still to this day I struggle with envy towards it. The Shelby Cobra. You can't deny the magnificence of such a beastly vehicle. I don't remember how it happened, but I remember my mother and his mother having to pry my hand open when they saw that I was obviously trying to hide something. I acted like it was an accident; I somehow even convinced myself that it was, but it was quite the embarrassing lesson.

Walking in God's will has no equal when it comes to the human experience

One of the things I've learned since then is that open hands allow God's plans. Try something with me; grab the nearest thing that you can in one hand, possibly a pen or cup. Now, grasp it tightly. Use the other hand to find another object and attempt to put it in the clenched hand. It doesn't work. Now try the same experiment, but keep the first hand open, palm up, and allow yourself to remove or stack objects.

God wants to put more in your hands; sometimes it will be additional things, and sometimes He will take something out to make room for the next thing. If you hold onto your position, power, or pride too tightly, then you will never get to experience anything past them. And there is so much more than those things. *Walking in God's will has no equal when it comes to the human experience.* That's because it is a supernatural relationship that protends anything this world can offer.

> *"He also who had received the one talent came forward, saying, 'Master, I knew you to be a hard man . . . so I was afraid, and I went and hid your talent in the ground. Here, you have what is yours.' But his master answered him, 'You wicked and slothful servant!' . . . And cast the worthless servant into the outer darkness. In that place there will be weeping and gnashing of teeth.'"*
> *—Matthew 25:24-26, 30*

If you prefer a different analogy, consider the Tarzan metaphor: to swing from rope to rope, you have to eventually let go of one. If you don't, you'll end up stranded, suspended in space with nowhere to go but down.

P. S. I have a Shelby Cobra now, a few of them actually, and I do play with them occasionally, along with my other Hot Wheels cars.

The Refinery

"Blessed are the pure in heart, for they shall see God."
—Matthew 5:8

This is a promise I hold to dearly. I desire to see God, to see Him again, to see something new in Him that I've never experienced before, to see Him work, to see His hand over my life and the lives of others, to see Him be who He is. And the Bible plainly lays out this stipulation: *to see God, we must strive to be pure.* You know that this doesn't happen as easily as it rolls of the tongue in the midst of so many powerful verses, another immensely rich scripture buried in the beatitudes that you may have recited monotonously as a child.

To see God, we must strive to be pure

Don't you want to see God? Don't you want people to know that you were with Him, and He with you? Then ask for his consuming fire to purify you. Ask for His Son to once again pass over you in order that He would be seen in you.

"And they recognized that they had been with Jesus."
—Acts 4:13b

There is a process that shows this beautifully: the refining of silver. Silver ore is mined from the earth, just as you came from earth, broken and impure with a sinful nature. It is put into a vat, or crucible, and heated. Eventually impurities, called dross (what a great name), come to the surface. Vanity, selfishness, pride, ambitions, arrogance, jealousy, spite, and so much more are shown to us through various trials. As you allow God to remove that wretched dross, you become more pure. The more pure the silver is, the more clearly the refiner can see his reflection in it. You are to be a mirror image of God, so you must allow His fire and guidance to remove the dross, so that when people see you, they see God. *They will know that you have been with God because your face will shine with His visage and presence.*

> *"The crucible is for silver, and the furnace is for gold,*
> *and the Lord tests hearts."*
> *—Proverbs 17:3*

> *"And I will put this third into the fire,*
> *and refine them as one refines silver,*
> *and test them as gold is tested.*
> *They will call upon my name,*
> *and I will answer them.*
> *I will say, 'They are my people';*
> *and they will say, 'The Lord is my God.'"*
> *—Zechariah 13:9*

"Take away the dross from the silver,
and the smith has material for a vessel."
—Proverbs 25:4

"Behold, I have refined you, but not as silver;
I have tried you in the furnace of affliction."
—Isaiah 48:10

"But we all, with unveiled face, beholding as in a mirror
the glory of the Lord, are being transformed into the same
image from glory to glory, just as by the Spirit of the Lord."
—2 Corinthians 3:18 (NKJV)

Get Over the Sun

In the creative world, we are always being reminded that nothing is new. Everything is inspired by something else or closely mimics another idea. Solomon saw this all that time ago, so even *then*, he said, "There is nothing new under the sun" (Ecc. 1:9). Often times when someone shares an idea or recognizes that we are copying another church's creative elements, he or she will say pretentiously, "There's nothing new under the sun." I've defaulted to that anecdote several times without considering the negativity that it carries. It can be a dream killing statement *if* we see it that way.

> *"Do not be conformed to this world, but be transformed by the renewing of your mind, that by testing you may discern what is the will of God, what is good and acceptable and perfect."*
> *—Romans 12:2*

It's time to get over the sun! The natural world is limited, our flesh has its own capacities. We are maxed out. According to the law of conservation of matter, matter cannot be created or destroyed. This implies that there is nothing now that has not always been, in some way, shape, or form. However, it can only be redirected or repurposed (see the Back Pocket Devo on Repurposers).

Nothing new can occur on this earth without God's divine hand. God speaks of *newness* all over His holy word. However, it always seems to be in direct connection to Him, the supernatural, the one who operates in the world but also outside of it.

We experience renewal daily when we trust in God and allow Him to change us from the inside out. I thank God that I'm not the same person I was last year, or even yesterday, Lord willing! And I believe that, while our services may not seem to carry any new themes or creative elements, in the grand scheme of things, we do have the opportunity to experience something new every time the doors open. That comes only from our God.

> We experience renewal daily when we trust in God and allow Him to change us from the inside out

In planning and preparation for upcoming events, we should throw away that "nothing new" statement unless we use it to point to God's limitless propensity for bringing His newness in whatever way He sees fit.

"And I will give you a new heart, and a new spirit I will put within you. And I will remove the heart of stone from your flesh and give you a heart of flesh."
—*Ezekiel 36:26*

"Therefore, if anyone is in Christ, he is a new creation. The old has passed away; behold, the new has come."
—*2 Corinthians 5:17*

"And to put on the new self, created after the likeness of God in true righteousness and holiness."
—Ephesians 4:24

"And have put on the new self, which is being renewed in knowledge after the image of its creator."
—Colossians 3:10

Purpose-full

Since May is a month of creation among the natural world, this month's topics center around allowing God to spark some creative ways for you to use these truths and inspire your weekly services, processes, volunteers, and attenders.

It's appropriate that Mother's Day falls in the beginning of a month when life is sprouting up all around you. When that day comes, I challenge you to lean into the message your pastor or leadership brings rather than this devotional. Do read the corresponding weeks, but I wouldn't recommend sharing them with your mother.

That's not what this is for. Let that day be about her and for her. Regardless of how you feel about her, she is also one of God's children. He loves her so much and wants her to know Him even more. This is true for all of His children, but let Him remind you of that on Mother's Day of all days.

At the time of writing this book, my mother has survived nearly 2 years of Stage 4 brain cancer, glioblastoma multiforme (GBM). She has gone through so much that I'll never really know about. My father has been beside her every step of the way. To be honest, she and I have had some difficult times. We are very similar in that we speak our minds. We both seem to believe that having the truth out there, regardless of how painful, is better than the alternative of holding it in and letting those things create communication-halting barriers. When others used to let her say or do whatever she wanted, I would speak up. Since the cancer though, I have found wisdom in extending grace to those moments. While I don't always hold my tongue, I do my best now to choose our battles. There are times to confront, but on Mother's day, or significant moments in her life, I choose to give her what she wants, no matter the cost. You won't regret that at the end of the day. What you will regret is the argument you started over where you went to eat or how long we all took to decide. You will regret looking at her faults and not celebrating the woman she is and the one God created her to be. You will have regrets regardless, but make the choices now that will remind her that she did something right with you and by God's grace.

Having a son now, I know that I will always love him and be proud of him. I also know that I will push him past his comfort zones on multiple occasions. I fight the fear that I will do the wrong thing from time to time, but I ultimately trust that God's grace will cover that. I will do my best to always point to His love and grace more than His warnings and wrath. When we turn our eyes upon Jesus, as the old hymn beautifully says, "The things of earth will grow strangely dim, in the light of His glory and grace." I hope to point to Him so much that my son sees the riches of God's love as more valuable that anything this earth has to offer. I hope to have a light shine—not only in me, but through me—so my son will experience God more than he experiences me. For even though I know I am a saint saved by grace, I struggle, and I make poor decisions occasionally, perhaps more than I'm even aware of. So if I point to myself, my son will be living for failure. *But if I point to my God through Christ, my son will have the ultimate role model.*

But if I point to my God through Christ, my son will have the ultimate role model

Your mother feels this way too, even though she may not know how to say it. Yes, she will take credit for more than she probably should, but she did give up a lot for you. She may not recognize that it was God all along and His strength being made known in her weakness. But you can recognize it, and you can celebrate God through her. Praise her for the amazing things you've gotten to experience in life because of God working through her. Let her know that you listened, learned, and loved. You would not have first known love if it weren't her choosing to help bring you into this world, and she would not have known love if it weren't for God as love himself.

Another holiday coming this month is Memorial Day. Memorial Day is just one of the handful of holidays across the culture that helps create the wonderful, highly celebrated 3-day weekend. For churches, however, it's not so glorious. Numbers fall, the volunteer base gets thin, everyone loosens up a bit, and we almost chock it up as a by-weekend. However, these services carry some of the most potential of any weekend. Since people are traveling, there are quite often guests in town who will visit your church. While they may not become members due to geography, they will carry with them what they've experienced, whether it's positive or not. Two types of people will come, those who need God and know they find more of Him there and those who just want to see what you're all about. This is a chance to satisfy everyone.

Don't let such weekends flatten your sails. Instead, set your sails, read the wind, and expect it to come powerfully. Let the culture around you become a driving factor for weekend preparation and execution rather than an excuse to phone it in. In whatever capacity you participate in, remember that this is kingdom work!

What you have to look forward to this month:

- Thoughts and challenges with creativity

- Your source and your legacy

- Inspiration to act, to be passionate

Creative with a Cause

"In the church, art is a wonderful servant but a terrible master."
—Stephen Miller

"Since the days of Pentecost, has the whole church ever put aside every other work and waited upon Him for ten days, that the Spirit's power might be manifested? We give too much attention to method and machinery and resources, and too little to the source of power."
—Hudson Taylor

Have you ever taken something too far? Specifically in reference to some creative element. As an artist, creator, and dreamer made in the image of the ultimate Artist, Creator, and Dreamer, you tend to think outside of the box. I was just recently told that I live outside of the box!

That's a beautiful, yet painful, place to be. Your heart yearns for what's new, unseen, and uncharted, which also means untested. Nothing is new to the world, but there are countless things that are new to you and your congregation. You have passions to chase them. You have the creative means to get outside of the box and look at things from a different perspective. To be useful and to grow in that, you must grow towards the source of it all, you must grow towards God.

> *"Delight yourself in the Lord, and he will
> give you the desires of your heart."*
> *—Psalms 37:4*

There is a providential, universal will for everyone: to bring glory to God. There is also a specific will for each that God wants to reveal in time. *God wants to use your passions more than you do.* But to know those passions, you must follow the order the verse speaks: delight *first*, and *then* He will give. Often this happens as He brings your desires in line with His desires or those He has for you.

> *"The way in which God fulfills a desire may be different from what first
> awakened it."*
> *—John Eldredge, Wild at Heart*

He has planted passions in your hearts that will ultimately glorify Him but also fulfill you in ways you never thought possible. So what brings life to your innermost being? What stirs your soul, ignites your heart, makes you feel as though your life is wasted without it? If the fuse has been lit, what is it you feel you must do before the explosion? As 2 Timothy 1:6 says, "fan into flame the gift of God," and do so without fear.

What things do you think about that also match the eighth verse of Philippians 4: *true, honorable, just, pure, lovely, commendable, of excellence or worthy of praise.* God put those desires there. He has plans deeper and wider than we could imagine, yet also more intricate and interwoven.

- Maybe that Instagram post about a concert, or some well-crafted hashtag, gets someone's attention and they follow you. Now you have a platform to share something encouraging to new followers.
- Maybe you meet someone because they like your shoes; you could befriend them and eventually invite them to church where God could do an amazing work in their lives, all because you were not only open to but seeking after God's direction in your life. Yes, even in buying shoes!
- Maybe someone sees that there is something different about you because you somehow live in passionate fulfillment; when they ask what it is, you'll have a chance to share the life-changing gospel of Christ!

Life lived apart from God will be meaningless, regardless of education, fulfilled goals, the greatest of pleasures, and the greatest abundance of wealth. Solomon, the wisest man ever, experienced everything this world has to offer and found that it is all *vanity*, useless, like chasing the wind. There is nothing to be gained from this world. However, it is through Christ, who is not of this world, where you find your worth, your purpose, your gain.

Life lived apart from God will be meaningless

> *"It is certain that man never achieves a clear knowledge of himself unless he has first looked upon God's face."*
> —*John Calvin*

Fuel This Fire

God will give you the desires of your heart if you first delight yourself in Him. And in drawing nearer to Him, He will help expose what those desires truly are.

- He has put a coal in your soul; apply some heat (the Word, time with God) and it will begin to smolder.

- Apply some oxygen (Holy Spirit's guidance-inspiration-breath-words from God) and smoke will protend.

- After you have done so, the fire is lit and will remain aglow with a little care and constant attention, staying with those original accelerants (time with God and hearing from the Holy Spirit; walking in the Spirit is part of His will for you)

> *"If we live by the Spirit, let us also walk by the Spirit."*
> *—Galatians 5:25*

- That fire inside of you will spread to everything you do.

- You will be consumed with a holy purpose that fulfills and consumes you in ways that you never knew it could.

- Chase those dreams! The ones you know are from God. Hold Him to His word and see if He won't fulfill you.

- Let yourself be the creative person God is creating you to be, one day at a time!

"This fire was lit by Your love,
Overcome by Your grace
I submit all I am.
Won't You fill my life with faith?
Wreck my heart, tear down my pride.
Use Your love to fuel this fire."

Remnants

> "... when the morning stars sang together
> and all the sons of God shouted for joy"
> —Job 38:7

Stars fascinate me. They send pulsating light of varying intensities over vast, unimaginable distances. We think of them as sending it directly to us, only to be seen hundreds of thousands of years later. To reconcile this with the Biblical creation timeline, we can assume that God created the universe with age as He seemed to have done with Adam, if that's preferable.

That light is more powerful than we think. It isn't just a concentrated beam sent to us. Light from a star is sent out spherically, which means in every single direction. Imagine that power. Oh, the beauty of that experience: each moment of light we soak in from a star is dying light as well as living light. That star is potentially dead already, burned up or dulled out by now. But its light is still impactful. It burned so brightly and powerfully that it left remnants of itself. Or perhaps it's still alive and firing in every direction. It's still known, felt, and appreciated by those who really experience its light. That is what it has to offer, and it offers it with all that it is.

We all want to be stars. But we should also consider traits of planets. Planets are made of rock or ice, sometimes gas, but don't burn of their own volition. In fact, they would be nearly invisible if it weren't for the stars near them. They, however, like the moon does the sun, reflect starlight from their nearest and most powerful source.

Luke 19:40 says that the stones will cry out. Creation cries out. Men with hearts of stone experience conversion and praise Him. The planets of rock orbit as constant reminders of His magnitude and power. If you seek to be a star, do it only so that what light God burns in you will be of Him and for Him, that your remnant will be that of a person after God's heart. Create, participate, invigorate, inspire, encourage something greater than you that will outlive you, that will become a beacon of light, that continues to travel and impact after you're gone. Be like the moon, reflecting the Son. *Be so near to Him that He will be the brightest thing people see from you.*

> **Be so near to Him that He will be the brightest thing people see from you**

"Praise him, sun and moon,
praise him, all you shining stars!"
—Psalms 148:3

Just Do It!

I'm not talking about that swooshy shoe brand. No, in the words of a great philosopher of our time, Shia LeBouf, I encourage you to "Just do it! Do it! Just . . . (aggressive finger point) . . . do it!"

> *"Ever tried. Ever failed. No matter.*
> *Try Again. Fail again. Fail better."*
> *—Samuel Beckett*

> *"Failure is success in progress."*
> *—Einstein*

> *"I've failed over and over again in my life.*
> *That is why I succeed."*
> *—Michael Jordan*

As an inventor, Edison had thousands of unsuccessful attempts while inventing the light bulb. Henry Ford failed and went broke five times before he succeeded. In high school, Robin Williams was voted "Least Likely to Succeed." Abraham Lincoln was demoted in war, from captain to private; failed at business and law; and was defeated time and time again in his attempts for various political elections. He felt the pain that you may feel, likely to a much greater degree. Here's what he wrote in the midst of it, "I am now the most miserable man living. If what I feel were equally distributed to the whole human family, there would not be one cheerful face on the earth."

That depression is common for great men.

Solomon, the wisest man on earth, held nothing back from himself from riches to accomplishments and women to all satisfactions he could find. After all of that, he found all things of earth to be as useless as chasing the wind; he alluded to the fact that the greatest thing you could do is enjoy the journey because every destination depressed him. He seemed to find the most fulfillment in finding joy in the work.

> *"So I saw that there is nothing better than that a man should rejoice in his work, for that is his lot. Who can bring him to see what will be after him?"*
> *—Ecclesiastes 3:22*

Find your joy in the work, in the mundane, in the day-to-day. *Find a way to embrace your path, to have joy in the journey.* Learn to enjoy using your tools. Learn that seemingly ancient art of craftsmanship, taking pride in each artistic or productive stroke.

"But it does require the supernatural grace of God to live twenty-four hours of every day as a saint, going through drudgery, and living an ordinary, unnoticed, and ignored existence as a disciple of Jesus. It is ingrained in us that we have to do exceptional things for God—but we do not. We have to be exceptional in the ordinary things of life, and holy on the ordinary streets, among ordinary people —and this is not learned in one hour."
—Oswald Chambers

Hey June

Churches will sometimes claim summer as a *slow* season. Ha! I wish I knew what a slow season at church really felt like. It's always crazy, in the best ways, at our church. We do so many things at such a high level of excellence that we convince ourselves that we can do more. Interesting logic, eh?

The truth is that anything good is from God, so it's arrogant to think that you are to be credited for His work. However, as you honor Him with your work, He keeps His hand on what you put your hands on.

Whether it's summer small groups, a stronger focus on the team and discipleship, extra events, a movie series, more new songs, holiday celebrations, unique service designs, or some other exciting addition, remember that renewable, reliable strength comes from Him, not others, not yourself, not even your family. Enjoy the lunacy, the variety, any ridiculousness, and the hustle. These are some of the days you'll look back on and miss. You always remember things better than they were. As time moves on, memories grow sweeter. Do your best to start them off well.

What you have to look forward to this month:

- Church vs. culture

- The power of passion

- Why 30/30 is actually great vision

- Lessons from a tree

American Idol Society

Anything good in my life is not natural.

When you see something good, a gifting or talent in someone, and it seems to come naturally, it doesn't. It's supernatural; it's from God.

As a Christ-follower who has the Holy Spirit living inside, you have a supernatural anointing from God Himself as well as spiritual gifts. Even those without Christ who seem to possess supernatural gifts still got them from God. He created them, formed them in their mother's womb, made them into masterpieces, and instilled passions, drives, abilities, inclinations, aptitudes, and more.

So when you see someone excelling, glorify God for what He chose to endow them with. And when the opposite happens, someone struggles to play or sing the right parts or flow with the band, have grace; but mostly remember that it is about Jesus and nothing else. *Just point to Jesus, always and in every circumstance.* Our "American Idol" society is so focused on performance. And as such, society often glorifies talents above people, ability above fortitude, and spotlights above service.

> Just point to Jesus, always and in every circumstance

I love leading with every one of my team members: band, vocalists, production, and more. And since my church has three growing campuses and more to come, members will alternate and cycle through weekend to weekend. Truthfully, you will have favorite musicians you play with, but in heaven, you may not even know the angels' names. You won't have a preference to worship alongside Michael rather than Gabriel. You should love singing with them now, angels and humans alike: because *it's not about the music you play, it's about the God you worship*. If you struggle with this, take yourself back to your early days, and recognize the grace God has extended and continues to extend over you.

If you have an overwhelming self-interest of looking good or sounding great, get rid of it! Ask God for help in that, and rest in the hope that you will be truly useful to Him in whatever way He wants. Who else in this world would you rather have the favor of? Who else would you rather impress and please? What benefit would it be to discard God's favor and plan for something you think is good? What do you know? What do you know that the God of the galaxies doesn't?!

> *"Turn your eyes upon Jesus,*
> *Look full in His wonderful face,*
> *And the things of earth will grow strangely dim,*
> *In the light of His glory and grace."*
> *—H. H. Lemmel, 1922*

Contagious

> *"To play a wrong note is insignificant but to play without passion is inexcusable."*
> —*Beethoven*

Some of the most powerful advice I've ever received was inspired by Galatians 6:7, which says that "God is not mocked." That also means that God will not be mocked. He will not allow it. *You have been charged with a great task: to lead people into battle.* You carry a heavier weight than most, yet Christ calls His burden light, as long as you trust Him to lead you. So when you lead, participate in worship services, or plan for events, let the Holy Spirit lead you first and foremost. You can't be faulted for that!

You have been charged with a great task: to lead people into battle

Don't let the congregation lead you. I know the feeling; the countdown ends, and you welcome everyone, all seven people (each of whom you know by name), to stand and clap or sing along. It can be deflating, but that's when you must ask yourself what you're doing and why you're doing it. You have the calling, the responsibility, the privilege to be in this position at this time for reasons known and unknown. If you let that get to you, you need to take some time to get alone with God, get your focus right again, and understand the call. Also, remember that all seven of those people have stories of their own, battles to face, and needs; this is where they've come for those answers, whether they're expectant or not.

Occasionally though, you'll be at an event that is maxed out, where the expectation in the building is palpable. Enjoy those moments when it's packed and people are participating with abandon. That's a move of God, not something you can orchestrate and reproduce. *However, it doesn't matter if it's five or five thousand, God is worthy* of all the praise you can bring Him and more, all the passion you can produce, all the might you can muster, all the strength you have.

*"Yours, O Lord, is the greatness and the power
and the glory and the victory and the majesty, for all that is
in the heavens and in the earth is yours. Yours is the kingdom,
O Lord, and you are exalted as head above all.
—1 Chronicles 29:11*

*"Great is the Lord, and greatly to be praised,
and his greatness is unsearchable."
—Psalms 145:3*

*"Worthy are you, our Lord and God,
to receive glory and honor and power,
for you created all things,
and by your will they existed and were created."
—Revelations 4:11*

*"I give thanks to you, O Lord my God, with my whole heart,
and I will glorify your name forever."
—Psalms 86:12*

30/30 Vision

A group of rhinoceroses (shouldn't that be rhinoceri?) is called a "crash." Rhinos can only see about thirty feet in front of them and can run up to thirty miles per hour. When a crash begins to charge, moving at full speed in untamable recklessness, they can't see far enough ahead to trust where they're going or even to course-correct. I think that is a beautiful design by God. We should let our worship be like a crash of rhinos: a passionate pursuit, a fearless fervor, a committed charge into battle. (McManus, *The Barbarian Way*)

When you sing, two of your heart-callings collide: your love of God and of music. Here, you get to embrace both obsessions. You should not waste it, but rather call on it as you sing.

The world will say, "You get what you pay for" or "What you put in is what you get out." In God's economy, it's not fair like that. What you put in comes back multiplied! When you lay what you love at His feet, He returns a fulfillment that far outweighs your *sacrifice*.

Passion is contagious; it's isn't something that is taught, it's something that is caught. Go forward with this challenge: *don't worship in the way you feel you should. Worship in the way that God desires*: dancing, shouting, unashamedly proclaiming His love and truth, as untamable as a crash of rhinos. Let it be contagious as you lead people to the fertile place of preparation for the work of the Holy Spirit.

> Don't worship in the way you feel you should. Worship in the way that God desires

*"Never be lacking in zeal, but keep your
spiritual fervor, serving the Lord."*
—Romans 12:11 (NIV)

Ground-Breaking

"Blessed is the man
who walks not in the counsel of the wicked,
nor stands in the way of sinners,
nor sits in the seat of scoffers;
but his delight is in the law of the Lord,
and on his law he meditates day and night.
He is like a tree
planted by streams of water
that yields its fruit in its season,
and its leaf does not wither.
In all that he does, he prospers."
—Psalms 3:1-3

There is wisdom in the trees there, standing strong, steady, and still
It's like they know some secret, ask them to tell and they will
They'll say, "You are ground-breaking a little each day
You are in the making, in every single way"
Branches and leaves reach for the Sun
They know that it holds their lives
Roots remain deep and dig further
They sway with the wind throughout time
Hold firm to the ground, there's provision all around
Though the days seem to move so slowly. There is life in
the stillness and growing is endless. One day you'll look
down and know this: that you are ground-breaking a little
each day. And you are in the making, in every single way.

Do you see the tree? How massive it is? It wasn't always that old, wise, and powerful post. Like a vibrant tree that started from the death of a seed, your leadership blooms from the death and dying of your wordly precepts. Sometimes it's in the quiet, and often it's in the storms. To become the pillar of strength that you hope to be one day, you'll have to consistently break ground, weather all types of seasons, wait through the drudgeries, have grace with the wind, hold firm to the law of the Lord, stand tall all through the days and nights, seek nourishment from the Son, strengthen your roots, wait patiently for what's to come, and embrace the *ringing* of His love inside you, year after year.

"At the timberline where the storms strike with the most fury, the sturdiest trees are found."
—Hudson Taylor

"The righteous flourish like the palm tree
and grow like a cedar in Lebanon.
They are planted in the house of the Lord;
they flourish in the courts of our God.
They still bear fruit in old age;
they are ever full of sap and green,
to declare that the Lord is upright;
He is my rock, and there is no unrighteousness in Him."
—Psalms 92:12-15

III. The Fight Against Flesh
Get Over Your SELF

Selfishness: the story is bigger than you, and it's not about you.

Envy: your focus shouldn't be on another person, it's not about him or her either.

Lust: what you live for should not be things of this world, you are created for more.

Fallacies: you don't know it all, your philosophies have holes, but God's Word is infallible, perfect, and true.

Satan, or Lucifer, had pride, thinking he was equal with God or at least deserving of more than he had. He was struck from heaven immediately (see Revelation 12, Ezekiel 28, Isaiah 14). There is no room for pride in God's kingdom. Oh, it is only by mercy and grace that such justice does not befall us. Praise God that he loves us enough to help us through our own pride. It is pride that is at the root of all that stands against our God and His truths.

> *"As it is, you boast in your arrogance.*
> *All such boasting is evil."*
> *—James 4:16*

> *"Look at the proud!*
> *They trust in themselves,*
> *and their lives are crooked.*
> *But the righteous will live*
> *by their faithfulness to God."*
> *—Habakkuk 2:4*

It is a battle every time I get on a stage to lead worship, sing, play music, speak, or more. Often, part of the battle is with myself, my flesh. I have pride that comes with my abilities and experiences. God has walked me through a lot of this. Now, instead of pride, it is more often confidence in His calling that I carry. However, there is always the possibility, the reality actually, that pride is riding on the coattails of that confidence, ready to jump up and take over if I ease my guard or forsake God's truth in the moment. I still fight it when things go well while leading, when I hear the comments and praise from people, or read the comments and see the videos they share on social media. I know I'm not alone in that. It's a natural progression of humanity to praise what we find attractive.

One of my favorite quotes comes from the movie, *The Secret Life of Walter Mitty* (check out week 3 of August for more): "Beautiful things don't ask for attention." If you've noticed, they don't need it either, but they still get it. They don't look for it. They don't live for it. They just exist and life comes near. Think about where people live, what draws them to certain destinations. Rivers, landscapes, oceans, mountains; these attract people. People move close to these things. When people have land and want to build a house, they don't just put the foundation anywhere. They are drawn to the most scenic areas, the place with the best view, the things of beauty.

When a person has attractive qualities, others are drawn to him or her as well. *Have you considered that just as God created the mountains of which we marvel to see His magnificent moldings, He created people with beauty so that we would recognize His greatness?* Those who are mature enough will glorify God through what they do. Many, however, will see their accomplishments as precisely that, theirs, not His.

We should work hard to point to God in all that we do; living a life that does so will automatically redirect the glory back to its source. When someone celebrates us, we should be kind, but not let it sink in to our soul. Attribute it to God. This doesn't have to be vocal every time, but it should be recognized internally at least.

We are at war with ourselves, but it's not as simple as North vs. South. It's not civil, it's not pretty, and it's not easily navigated. However, we have battle plans drawn out in His word. Hold fast to those truths and stay alert. *The enemy also knows the plan and will ambush us at our weakest points and try to redirect our charge in his favor.*

> *"Do nothing from selfish ambition or conceit, but in humility count others more significant than yourselves."*
> *—Philippians 2:3*

> *"Do not love the world or the things in the world. If anyone loves the world, the love of the Father is not in him. For all that is in the world—the desires of the flesh and the desires of the eyes and pride of life—is not from the Father but is from the world. And the world is passing away along with its desires, but whoever does the will of God abides forever."*
> *—1 John 2:15-17*

> *"But he gives more grace. Therefore it says, "God opposes the proud but gives grace to the humble." Submit yourselves therefore to God. Resist the devil, and he will flee from you. Draw near to God, and he will draw near to you. Cleanse your hands, you sinners, and purify your hearts, you double-minded. Be wretched and mourn and weep. Let your laughter be turned to mourning and your joy to gloom. Humble yourselves before the Lord, and he will exalt you."*
> *—James 4:6-10*

And as always, consider Christ:

> *"For he grew up before him like a young plant,*
> *and like a root out of dry ground;*
> *he had no form or majesty that we should look at him,*
> *and no beauty that we should desire him."*
> *—Isaiah 53:2*

There was something else about Him, something that shown brightly from the inside out, something that couldn't be explained by the laws of nature. You, as a Christian, have that, the light of Christ. When people say to you, "There's just something different about you, something special," they are recognizing Christ in you. When people compliment your beauty or talent, they are experiencing God's creation. When people look at you with admiration, remember that it is Christ in you whom they admire, whether they know it or not. If you are attractive physically, He made you that way and also in His image. If you are smiling, they are experiencing joy or peace from God. When you sing notes with purity and perfect pitch, it's God who made that possible by giving you fortitude, passion, and drive. *Don't take credit for Christ. Direct it back to Him in a life of praise.*

Don't take credit for Christ. Direct it back to Him in a life of praise

God Uses Us in Amazing Ways

Let me share this story with you. It's tough, but there is purpose in it, especially if you sing or serve on stage. You may never know what God is up to, but it's always good.

Greyson Dickson (6/11/15 – 9/30/15)

My wife, Ashton, and I had the privilege of playing for a funeral for an infant who died of SIDs (Sudden Infant Death) in 2015. Later, they found out that it was acute onset of bronchial pneumonia. Ashton was specifically requested to sing by the mother, Darlen, and I accompanied on guitar for the afternoon. I think I took a late lunch break from work at the college in order to help. The funeral was actually on Ashton's birthday, which was a strange juxtaposition to navigate. On top of that, we were actually about seven months into trying to get pregnant, succeeding just a month later.

I don't remember the songs we sang, perhaps "Not for a Moment" by Meredith Andrews and another worship song from our weekend experiences. I don't remember what we did the rest of that day. I don't remember much about the service except for the deep sadness that day. We all try to have joy, but God gave us the full gamut of emotion so that we could experience all of it, and so that each opposite would be even stronger.

I just went back to her Facebook feed and followed her son's first and only three months of pictures. I noticed the same chalkboard announcements chronicling each month and its milestones that we did for our own son. I can't imagine not having that subsequent "4 Months Old" board for our little Nathan. God has some amazing plans for that family, but it hurts. It still hurts. We can't act like it doesn't or hasn't. That's not what He expects either. God the Father went through pain as His Son suffered and died, and we find life in that remembrance.

The pain may never go away for such events and losses, and the reasons aren't always revealed to you in this lifetime. In remembering Christ, it serves to remind you of the sacrifice that was necessary. It reminds you that God has a plan bigger than the moment, bigger than your 3 months or 90 years. Be glad that you get to be a part of it in whatever capacity. You and I are not worthy of this, apart from Christ, but He has chosen to use you where you are. Don't waste it. Don't mistreat it. Don't take the call to battle lightly. It's no small thing to stand, ready or not, at the frontline, no matter what may come. Don't squander your gifts. Don't mock God by taking them into your own hands. Don't let your flesh rule your spirit. Let God rule all of you so that you may be of utmost use to Him.

I'm getting to the point, I promise!

Ashton has had a hard time lately because she hasn't been able to serve on the worship team much since our son was born. After being up there nearly every weekend for several years, it's been a challenge to step back, regardless of the reason. Well, she got to lead again around five months into our son's life, and DD was there. She wrote this note that night, just over a year after the funeral.

> *"Ashton,*
>
> *As I stood up front to pray with others, all I could do is focus on your sweet voice. When I was at my very lowest your voice brought me comfort that day.*

To hear you sing just overwhelms my spirit with love and joy. YOUR VOICE gave me a sense of peace when my whole world was falling to pieces. Tonight even as I prayed for a lady who came forward, my heart was weary. But the opportunity to pray for another and hear YOUR VOICE . . . my worries disappeared and was exchanged for pure joy. I worshipped tonight in a way I have never before. You matter so much more than you think. I just want to say THANK YOU and I have a love in my heart for you that will never be forgotten. I hope you have a MERRY CHRISTMAS!

Kiss that BABY for us!

Love You —,

Darlen"

I still tear up at that last part. *You may never know what impact your leadership and service has in someone's life.* Don't take it lightly.

Challenge Goes to the Leaders

Going into the late summertime is when you really reveal your leadership. In evaluating a year, a season, or even a service, you are only as strong as your weakest weekend. And when you are at the bare minimum of staffing and volunteers, that is where your leadership is exposed: good, bad, and ugly. Find those wobbly joints and fortify them. Use these opportunities when things are more exposed to troubleshoot and adjust. These weekends are arguably the most important to the longevity of your church. Your leadership, from whatever capacity, is tested and tried with the end goal being betterment. Don't leave the weekend discouraged, but rather encouraged that God had the grace to show you how you could better serve Him and His beloved bride, the church.

July is also a time of gearing up for the large numbers to come when school starts back. The famine will turn to feast at harvest time. To be ready for that, leadership structures must be ready to handle it. The foundations must be checked or reinforced. That means digging deep rather than wide. Setting the posts so that teams and systems can handle the weight of what's to come.

For worship leaders, you must maintain the health of your team, or work hard to ensure their stability. It gives you the chance to dig into the vision of worship and take people deeper. This is a great time to work on that culture, to get it going now so that August and September won't overwhelm with all the newness clashing with former expectations. This is the time to chase after God's heart in worship, to open up to whatever new challenges He places before you, and to lead with confidence into this new level of connection to Him. While the numbers may be low, it means that those showing up are hungry; they want more of God. They know they *need* more of Him. Use that expectancy to help build momentum.

You set the environment, you set the temperature. The level of your expectation is proportionate to the presence of God, or more specifically, the openness of His people to experience Him. While doing your part, expect and pray for God to be elevated, for Him to move, and for people to respond to Him and know Him more. There will be excitement at times, but don't let that be your driving factor. As a leader, you drive it. However many weeks in the year that you are there, respond with everything that you have, regardless of what it looks like on the other side.

> You set the environment, you set the temperature

What you have to look forward to this month:

- Where strength is when it feels lost

- How to keep moving

- What to do when you don't feel special

- The value of working together

Strength When There is None

I often question my energy level on and off the stage while worshiping. Often times, I feel I should hold back because I may not have enough strength to endure all of the services or sets I'm participating in. When I have that reservation, I reach out to God for wisdom and strength. I have learned that my strength is nothing without His. He has called me to worship him with *all* that I am! In moments when I consciously begin to hold back, I am reminded that He will provide what I need. If I am to lead His people, then I will do so with vigor, passion, reckless abandon, and I will focus less on my physical limitations and more on the joy of the Lord.

> *"And do not be grieved, for the joy of the Lord is your strength."*
> *—Nehemiah 8:10b*

The *joy* of the Lord is my strength! When I feel weak, tired, inadequate, I look to Him. He reminds me that He is in control, and that He will do with me what He wills. If He uses me up completely, so be it! When He takes me to the end of myself in every way, then I stop assessing those things. Instead, I allow the joy of knowing Him along with His Holy Spirit to empower me.

> *"The Lord is my strength and my shield; my heart trusts in him, and he helps me. My heart leaps for joy, and with my song I praise him."*
> *—Psalms 28:7 (NIV)*

So when you worship, give it all that you have and trust that God will provide when you feel you can't. Coaches say it all the time, "Leave it on the field!" Worship is so much bigger than your dreams and regrets, it's bigger than your strengths and weaknesses, it's bigger than your passions and reservations. Leave it on the stage, leave it in your chair, leave it in your closet; don't walk away with regrets thinking that you didn't give God your all. Remember, this is war, this is a battlefield, and God is equipping every soldier with His strength so that no emotional, spiritual, mental or physical limitation can stop you!

> *"And you shall love the Lord your God with all your heart and with all your soul and with all your mind and with all your strength."*
> *—Mark 12:30*

When You Just Can't

As I write, I am in one of the craziest and busiest times of my life thus far. I feel pulled in dozens of different directions daily. I hope that I'm being effective, but I feel as though I am only giving each task sixty percent or less. Someone recently encouraged me, saying that sixty percent from me, in the position I'm designed for, is better than ninety percent from someone else who isn't right for it. I only believe that because of Christ Himself working in me. *Where I feel my weakness gleams, His strength is being seen.*

> *"My grace is sufficient for you,*
> *for My strength is made perfect in weakness."*
> *—2 Corinthians 12:9 (NKJV)*

One of the reasons, if not the main one, for my scattered passions has been the birth and early months of my son's life. In these first four to five months, my world has been challenged in more ways than I could explain. God is teaching me so much, primarily that He is a God who provides.

> *"And my God will supply every need of yours*
> *according to his riches in glory in Christ Jesus."*
> *—Philippians 4:9*

A great fear of mine was losing myself to fatherhood, knowing I would redirect my passions and drive towards my son. But just as always, God takes something and flips it in the most beautiful way. I thought I would lose myself, but I am finding more of me than I ever knew there was. Maybe it's part of reaching the end of yourself; *when you look to Him and say, "I can't do this anymore," He says, "I can."* That's where He operates the most!

When you look to Him and say, "I can't do this anymore," He says, "I can."

Limitations

> *"Nothing will hold you back;*
> *you will not be overwhelmed.*
> *Always remember what you have been taught,*
> *and don't let go of it.*
> *Keep all that you have learned;*
> *it is the most important thing in life."*
> *—Proverbs 4:12-13 (NCV)*

Let nothing limit your worship. One of my good friends has some handicaps, as the world would call them, that he's had since birth. If you ask him, he doesn't let anything stop him from participating and fulfilling his passions. Often, if you tell him he can't do something, he will work harder to prove you wrong and to prove it to himself. His hands are deformed and smaller than normal, with only two fingers on one hand and four on the other. He doesn't have a right foot, but still has his leg.

He's one of our church's primary drummers. That's right. He has a prosthetic right foot, which operates the kick drum. He obviously has to work harder than other people, more equipped people, but that doesn't stop him. He occasionally has trouble gripping the drum sticks and has to reset his grip multiple times during the service. However, he is an exceptional drummer. Throughout his development, a few of us had reservations, but he has proved us wrong over and over again.

Like my friend, *sometimes God gives you passion in an area for which you are not equipped.* He overcame. By God's grace, this young man has been equipped with such passion and drive that he lets nothing hinder or limit his offerings to God in worship.

Sometimes God gives you passion in an area for which you are not equipped

I, too, have a handicap. When I was eleven, I lost my left eye to a lawn dart incident. Yep, I'm one of those statistics. And it happened at a church, of all places! So a small lesson there is that you can be in the right place and still suffer loss. God has bigger plans. My limitations are shallow. It affects the way I look physically; the prosthetic eye will never truly fit, appear, or function like a real eye. And the worst part, I can't truly experience 3-D movies! What's the point of life if I can't have that?!

At the risk of sounding hackneyed, God used this massive event in my life to give me a singular focus. Before one of my surgeries, a nurse told my mother that God had great plans for me. My mother told me that the rest of my life, and I believed it. I still do. It's true for each person breathing today.

"'For I know the plans I have for you,' says the Lord. 'They are plans for good and not for disaster, to give you a future and a hope. In those days when you pray, I will listen. If you look for me wholeheartedly, you will find me. I will be found by you,' says the Lord. 'I will end your captivity and restore your fortunes. I will gather you out of the nations where I sent you and will bring you home again to your own land.'"
—Jeremiah 29:11-14

(Extra) Ordinary

> *"Every artist was at first an amateur."*
> —*Ralph Waldo Emerson*

What do you do when you're born normal? Just an ordinary person with average talents watching the *extraordinary* people excel all around you. I've often landed in the average-to-above-average categories in life but hardly ever at the top of the list. I have to work hard in the areas in which I excel. And, through God's grace I am able to achieve much. So, know this, *you are not ordinary when God has His hand on you. You are holy, set apart for a greater purpose than you could design on your own.*

When you see people doing extraordinary things, try instead to see God doing those things *through* the people. And remember that they didn't start there. It takes time, effort, and commitment. Most of all, it takes obedience to the call of Christ to be part of His amazing work. The book of Joshua spoke of this, begging the people to dedicate themselves to God, to be consecrated for His call. Behind that request is the promise that they will see God do amazing things. Don't you want to see amazing things?!

> *"Consecrate yourselves, for tomorrow the LORD will do amazing things among you."*
> —*Joshua 3:5 (NIV)*

Collaborators, Not Competitors

"As part of Christ's army, you march in the ranks of gallant spirits. Every one of your fellow soldiers is the child of a King. Some, like you, are in the midst of battle, besieged on every side by affliction and temptation. Others, after many assaults, repulses, and rallying of their faith, are already standing upon the wall of heaven as conquerors. From there they look down and urge you, their comrades on earth, to march up the hill after them. This is their cry: Fight to the death and the City is your own, as now it is ours!"
—William Gurnall

You are not in a competition, nothing about church service is. The person to your right, left, ahead or behind, above or below is your brother, a fellow soldier for Christ. Would an honorable man in battle trip his compatriot in attempt to claim a better kill? There is a healthy sort of rivalry in brotherly love, when the object of competition is somewhat trivial. But in the larger scheme, if the competition is over souls or kingdom work, then the rivalry has gone too far.

We all have problems, but we're in this together! How does this constantly escape us? We are the church; let's be collaborators not competitors. Let's be cheerleaders and not the *away* team. Let's be what we claim to be: let's be family.

Family is tough. They've seen you at your worst. They've seen all the crappy versions of yourself that you wish no one knew about. And sometimes they still see the old *you* when you are the new *you*. But family also stands together, despite those terrible moments, and fights for each other. They may fight amongst themselves as well, but they don't usually leave, seeking a new family. That's ridiculous. Imagine getting upset with your parents and then just walking next door and saying, "I'd like to be in your family now; I don't like mine anymore." I know that's a loose allegory to church hopping; forgive me for the loopholes as I can't weave together perfect metaphors. I'm not Jesus.

So when one of us falls, let's all be honest and help them up. And when one of us excels or succeeds, let's all be honest and celebrate with them! Remember that each "win" (surely a buzzword at a church near you) is not a win for the individual but rather for the kingdom of God. Each worship service or song that is led effectively with fruitful return is adding to the kingdom in one way or another. Perhaps it's salvation in the room or more likely it inspires a current believer to step closer to God and further into the life He has planned for them; and it is in that life that God will be glorified, potentially bringing more lives to the saving knowledge of Christ. *Everything we get to do as worship leaders, vocalists, musicians, tech or production roles, guest services, campus pastors, and more has eternal significance, kingdom connection, potential power for God to put to use in whatever way He sees fit.*

> Everything we get to do has eternal significance, kingdom connection, potential power for God to put to use in whatever way He sees fit

The Rush of August

Even if you didn't use the summer as effectively as you'd hoped to, strive to lay down a solid foundation for worship; this season is still full of chances to start again. This month you may experience some of the most attended services of the year. When school starts back, schedules fall into place, and Sunday mornings aren't as easily forgotten or overlooked as they were in the summertime.

Your goal isn't to please every person who comes to your church, nor is it to change their lives. That's the Holy Spirit's work. Your job is simply to convey the gospel clearly. *Part of the gospel is that mysterious combination of grace and mercy, which exists on both sides of messing up.* Those who find mistakes in the services will either be reminded that no one is perfect, which is actually quite an encouraging thought, or they will judge it harshly and choose a different path. Again, that's not on you. So use this time to get creative while keeping the gospel at the forefront, and let God take it from there.

> Part of the gospel is that mysterious combination of grace and mercy, which exists on both sides of messing up

Let God be in charge, let Him prompt people's spirits, reminding them of something bigger and drawing them closer to those truths a little at a time, closer to Him. Music, especially when we're aware that it is God ordained, has a mysterious way of transcending your expectations.

> *"You know what music is? God's little reminder that there's something else besides us in this universe, a harmonic connection between all living beings, everywhere, even the stars."*
> —*Wizard, in August Rush*

What you have to look forward to this month:

- A cheesy and dated movie reference

- A proper way to say, "Thank you"

- A reference to one of my favorite movies

- A comparison of comparison: comparison squared

The Need to Lead

Do you feel the need? The need to lead? I know, I know, I'm leaning into the *Top Gun* fan base out there, all 8 of you. Think about it though. When a certain song hits the set list or a special moment is engineered in a service, do you vie for that spot? Or if you aren't a consideration, do you have your favorites that you prefer singing instead of others, maybe less talented people, getting the chance? Hold your horses, Maverick. When you do this, and we all do it, you are giving in to this *Idol* culture. You, or some other singer, may very well be the *best* vocalist for a specific song, but is talent the thing that God desires most? God gave you the talent, so of course He loves to have it returned; that's one of the bases for worship. However, the Bible does not speak of talent being primarily pleasing to God. It speaks of faith, spiritual mindedness, fear, obedience, sacrifice, having the mind of Christ, humility, and the like.

The old adage, "out of sight, out of mind" is still true, maybe even more so in the church. That's a worldly precept, not biblical at all. Matthew 20:16 says, "So the last will be first, and the first will be last." God celebrates humility. What a paradoxical thought?

Consider this: is it the show-boater who is the *best* kingdom builder? We would think, "Of course not!" But our actions say the opposite. *We put talent on display and worship excellence nearly as much as we worship God.* We celebrate talent in the church. That's not innately a bad thing. But when talent trumps commitment, spiritual maturity, a true heart of worship, the desire for God

> We put talent on display and worship excellence nearly as much as we worship God

to be glorified and not oneself, then we have failed, my friends. And we have all fallen, and in my experience, are still failing.

So what's the answer? Matthew 6:33 says, "Seek first the kingdom of God and his righteousness." When you recognize the world rising up in yourself, the need to lead, the need to be seen and heard, take it to God. Make the same request as the psalmist:

"And see if there is any wicked way in me,
And lead me in the way everlasting."
—Psalms 139:24

"For to set the mind on the flesh is death, but to set the mind
on the Spirit is life and peace. For the mind that is set on the flesh
is hostile to God, for it does not submit to God's law; indeed, it
cannot. Those who are in the flesh cannot please God."
—Romans 8:6-8

"Walk as children of light (for the fruit of light is found in all that is
good and right and true), and try to discern what is pleasing to the Lord."
—Ephesians 5:8b-10

He is Worthy

For anyone who has stage time, there's often that awkward moment when people compliment you after service. If you are often told that you did well, I would strongly urge you to reconsider your stage leadership style. Usually people compliment performances; therefore, they feel that is what they have witnessed. When people experience truer worship, they will thank you for *leading* them, or say something about the presence of God or your willingness to be used by Him. If those are the things you're hearing, well done!

The awkwardness comes when you feel pressured to respond in a way that is appropriate and God-honoring. However, in the moment, that's more difficult said than done. "Thank you" is often the best response, no need to expound upon it or treat it like a post-game interview: *"I worked hard, the whole team worked hard. I just wanna thank God, and my family. Also, Pastor gave us good direction, the congregation was really into it this time, so that always helps. The Holy Spirit showed up, always a good day when that happens. Yeah, I'm proud of what we were able to accomplish up there."*

I make light of this, but it's not far from the things we've actually said before. The primary issue here is that *we* are not to be credited for that which is good.

If anything is good, it is first from God, whether it be the work ethic that He helped cultivate in each of us or His guidance over the service and everyone involved. We can't lose sight that His hand is in every good thing that we experience, have experienced, or will experience.

If anything is good, it is first from God

Once, my wife ran into an older lady in the restroom (some of the best moments are steeped in awkwardness) and my wife said to her, "I'm so encouraged to see your worship." That lady was never on stage, but she still led worship in her own way, from the congregation. I was blown away when my wife shared her response: "He is worthy."

I feel that is one of the best responses because that lady gets it, to the core. Her first thought wasn't, "Yeah, *I* did worship whole-heartedly." No, it was, "He is the reason for anything good, He is the reason I worship, He alone is worthy of it."

> *"to him be glory in the church and in Christ Jesus throughout all generations, forever and ever. Amen."*
> —*Ephesians 3:21*

Beautiful Things

My wife has the most beautiful, angelic singing voice. When she leads worship, God arrests my heart and His grip brings tears to my eyes. I'm not just being biased; she is an amazing worship leader. However, she gets worked up when she is asked to sing a song in church that isn't a worship song, as if singing itself isn't worshipful. She feels it's a performance that puts the attention on herself. For the longest time, I agreed with her and even admired her value on the purity of worshiping our God through song. But I have a new perspective now.

Consider a field full of beautiful flowers, or a waterfall, perhaps a mountain, the ocean, or the stars. Or if you're an animal lover, or a movie fan you may remember, the Snow Leopard:

> *"Beautiful Things Don't Ask for Attention"*
> *— The Secret Life of Walter Mitty*

It is not some arrogance that demands attention. It is simply the beauty of the creation. God is responsible for that beauty. I've heard it said, "God is showing off" when it comes to such amazing things. I don't think so. I think God is being God. He creates, inspires, and breathes magnificence. It's not a grand effort, it's who He is.

So when my wife sings, I don't just see her beauty or get lost in her voice for her alone. No, I am reminded of how good God is, that He would give us such gifts to enjoy here on earth. I am reminded that *there is a heaven where such beauty runs rampant with no end.* I am reminded that He loves us so much, that He doesn't leave us stranded on this earth without promises and reminders of His goodness.

You exist to remind of God's glory, to point to a story bigger than we know

Get outside of yourself, outside of this idea of performing or not performing. Flowers simply are. A waterfall is falling water. The mountain just is. The ocean is being the ocean. The Snow Leopard exists in its own unique, intriguing way. The stars don't hold back. My wife sings; it's one of the things she's created to do. *You exist to remind of God's glory, to point to a story bigger than we know.*

Comparison

> *"Do nothing from selfish ambition or conceit, but in humility count others more significant than yourselves."*
> —*Philippians 2:3*

As a musician, and as a man, I was wrecked when the Holy Spirit revealed this verse to me. I had believed that competition led to greatness and that ambition was one of the pillars of life. Those things are often true in this world, but they are not ultimate, nor are they above biblical truths. I had to learn to put such things aside when it came to the worship of our God.

In comparing yourself to others of similar or different positions, ask yourself this question: *"Does their worship please God any less than mine?"* I hope you know the answer to that. For me, I choose to take competition elsewhere or avoid it altogether. *There is no room on God's stage for your ego.* When it comes to the stage, or some area of ministry or leadership, you should work hard to surrender your vanity and ambition to the moments God has designed. He doesn't need you, but He wants you. So focus on working together, as a family.

There is no room on God's stage for your ego

When one brother gets an opportunity to shine, don't question it or think, "I could do that, probably even better." When a sister sings an amazing solo, don't wish it were you. For some reason, God has allowed him or her to be in that position for that day and time. *If His message is being presented effectively, then all have reason to celebrate!* Encourage one another, be grateful that you get to experience those moments together.

"And above all these put on love, which binds everything together in perfect harmony. And let the peace of Christ rule in your hearts, to which indeed you were called in one body. And be thankful. Let the word of Christ dwell in you richly, teaching and admonishing one another in all wisdom, singing psalms and hymns and spiritual songs, with thankfulness in your hearts to God. And whatever you do, in word or deed, do everything in the name of the Lord Jesus, giving thanks to God the Father through him."
—Colossians 3:14-17

What Love Was and Is

September is one of my favorite months. It doesn't contain many holidays, but it does include both my wife's birthday and mine. Its latter days also mark the beginning of my favorite season: fall, or if you prefer, autumn, a season so good it gets two names.

When you see a tree, flower, plant or anything that was once a seed, can you find the seed anymore? No, it's gone, essentially dead. One day, your sinful man will be completely gone. Every day that you walk with Christ, parts of you are being replaced. Once you die physically, that sinful person you once were will be gone, dead.

Keep dying so that you can truly live.

Here's another perspective. Ben Rector, in his song "Autumn," sings about a leaf falling to the ground. He said that the leaf had to die to be found, and that is a representation of love. Be like the leaves, falling so they can be found; providing evidence of change; reminding you that new life is coming, the former life is gone, and seasons have reasons.

Keep dying so that you can truly live

> *"Truly, truly, I say to you, unless a grain of wheat falls into the earth and dies, it remains alone; but if it dies, it bears much fruit. Whoever loves his life loses it, and whoever hates his life in this world will keep it for eternal life."*
> *—John 12:24-25*

What you have to look forward to this month:

- Checking your I.D.

- A foggy lesson

- Wild worship

- The "not-so-secret" answer to life (no, it's not '42')

Insecurities

What is something you want to do but rarely get to do? Choose set lists, lead a song, play a specific part, design a light show, speak to a group of people, lead a moment, share your heart on a topic? Sometimes that thing is indicative of a larger issue, an insecurity that you have. You're allowing yourself to find identity in being a *lead* vocalist, rather than where it should be, in Christ alone. *When you trust that He is your sole purpose, other reasons fade away.*

> When you trust that He is your sole purpose, other reasons fade away

Sometimes it is about the season you're in. Or perhaps, whether you know it or not, you aren't ready in your talent level, leadership qualities, responsibility capacity, schedule, spiritual development, or more. Who knows? God does. He always knows better. As you struggle with these things, ask yourself, and be honest, *"Do I really think that I can imagine a better future for myself than God can?"* The answer is obvious, yet you still live as if you think you can. Imagine that your younger self got all of his or her wishes and dreams fulfilled, perhaps international stardom and worldly fulfillment. God knew better; He knew that you probably couldn't handle that lifestyle; He knew that you would most likely be full of despair, saturated with worldly passion, and empty and devoid of meaning. Praise God you are not that person! God knows your heart and your passions, present and future, and He has great plans for those things.

The enemy, however, also knows your passions, but only past and present. He knows your insecurities; he can spot them a mile away in anyone. He's been at this game for a long time, and there are only so many personality types out there. He's had thousands of years of practice. So he accuses and attacks those in the context of worship, whether it's from the platform or behind the scenes, or from the congregation or listening to the radio in the car. *Don't let the devil whisper identity to you.* He wants your heart, but he wants it so that God can't have it. He knows the power of a Christ-filled, Holy Spirit-focused, God-centered life, and it scares him.

> *"And I heard a loud voice in heaven, saying, 'Now the salvation and the power and the kingdom of our God and the authority of his Christ have come, for the accuser of our brothers has been thrown down, who accuses them day and night before our God. And they have conquered him by the blood of the Lamb and by the word of their testimony, for they loved not their lives even unto death. Therefore, rejoice, O heavens and you who dwell in them! But woe to you, O earth and sea, for the devil has come down to you in great wrath, because he knows that his time is short!'"*
> —Revelation 12:10-12

Fog

This morning, or sometime this month, you may have experienced one of my favorite things: a cool, foggy morning. There is something magical about it. I think it has to do with the fact that it makes your world feel so small and intimate while tickling the notions that so much more waits on the other side. There's mystery in the unknown, such amazing things could be happening, and most likely are happening somewhere in the mist.

Fog is what keeps us from seeing and experiencing all that the world has to offer. This promise of hidden treasure beckons. The closer we get to an object, the clearer it becomes. As we continue on our journey, we begin to see beautiful pieces of nature seemingly crawl through the hazy atmosphere. A tree, once completely covered, still exists whether we see it or not. When we get close enough to touch it, the fog thins out showing detail we could only have formerly imagined.

This is the same with Christ; as we draw near to Him, truth becomes more clear, we find things hoped for, we experience joy uninhibited, beauty becomes more vivid, and we get to experience that which exists beyond imagination, abundantly more than we can imagine.

Don't let the fog of life keep you from living to the fullest, from knowing our God in His infinite goodness, from worshiping in newness, and from discovering the immeasurable details of walking in His will.

*"We don't yet see things clearly. We're squinting in a fog,
peering through a mist. But it won't be long before the weather clears
and the sun shines bright! We'll see it all then, see it all as clearly
as God sees us, knowing him directly just as he knows us!"*
—1 Corinthians 13:12 (The Message)

Worship in the Wilderness

"When lonely meets the only One, and chaos finds a path.
From my flesh to the supernatural clearing of my past,
I will sing. I'll worship in the wilderness.
When wind and rain and fire hits every part of who I am, I will worship.
Where sin and pain and lies exist, I'll rest in Your arms.
I know where the quiet is, in the Savior's song."

Finding your way to worship can be daunting. You'll sometimes feel stranded, alone, vulnerable. When you step out of a place of comfort, your old boundaries are gone. New ones await, but you can't see them yet. It's a wild and wonderful world of exploration and challenge.

If you've never done this, it's not too late. *If you want to worship as the Lord wants you to, then you'll always be exploring and seeking Him out.* I don't think any of us are doing it right, not completely. But I know that moving closer to Him is always the answer.

> If you want to worship as the Lord wants you to, then you'll always be exploring and seeking Him out

When you are in that wilderness, or any other type of barbarian place, you can always find refuge in the Lord, a grace that He extends to you when you need Him most. You can rest in the Savior's song, the reminder of that great sacrifice because of the Lord's faithful and everlasting love.

> "Thus says the Lord:
> The people who survived the sword
> found grace in the wilderness;
> when Israel sought for rest,
> the Lord appeared to him from far away.
> I have loved you with an everlasting love;
> therefore I have continued my faithfulness to you.'"
> —Jeremiah 31:2-3

Come Closer

> *"Let us then with confidence draw near to the throne of grace,*
> *that we may receive mercy and find grace to help in time of need."*
> *—Hebrews 4:16*

I have found the answer to every question! It's definitely gonna be one of those no-brainers that leaves you saying, "Of course, but that doesn't really count, it doesn't answer *my* question."

Have you ever spent time with an older, wiser person? Usually it's a grandparent or family member. Occasionally, when you ask them a question, they lean in and beckon your presence by curling their fingers, palm up. It's a simple motion, but everyone knows what it means. Sometimes they give the obvious accompanying vocal instruction, "Come closer." You are forced to lean in if you truly want the answer.

That's it. That's the answer to every question you'll ever have in life. It's God calling you nearer to Him. It's God's entire will for your life.

"Which job should I take?"

"Come closer."

"How am I supposed to handle this situation, illness, turmoil, pain?"

"Come closer."

"Should I marry this person?"

"Come closer."

"I'm so angry with this person!" (This one intentionally follows the spouse question.)

"Come closer."

That's always the first step: draw nearer to God. To hear Him clearly, you must be close to Him. To feel Him and His presence, you must be close to Him. To see Him in detail, you must be close to Him. To know Him, you must be close to Him.

As you lean in, if you know the person well enough, you'll already have an idea of what they might say. As you lean in to God, you'll probably already know what He has to say about what you're bringing. All of this comes with an amazing promise, a guarantee:

> *"Draw near to God, and he will draw near to you."*
> *—James 4:8*

IV. The Fight with Leadership and Team Members

> *"Courage is what it takes to stand up and speak;*
> *Courage is also what it takes to sit down and listen."*
> —Winston Churchill

You're likely gearing up for fall festivals, season events, high and low weekend numbers, Thanksgiving, Christmas concerts, and more. Tensions are high and will likely get worse as the year crashes to an end. In a perfect world, you wouldn't have conflict at all. And you would hope it would be easier to work with others in the church than in the world. In some ways, it's so much better, but working with your fellow leaders and team members can still present challenges. It shouldn't feel like a fight, but it often does. First of all, if you see it this way, as a fight, then a change of perspective is needed, potentially on both sides. Notice the language in this section's title; the other sections were titled "the fight *against*" but this one reads "the fight *with*." You need to take those conflicts and realize they are ultimately not against each other. They are against the enemy, the flesh, or other circumstances. You fight with, or alongside, your friends and colleagues, your brothers and sisters, your leaders and volunteers.

A good soldier doesn't question his orders, he just follows the command

As you've discovered, worship is warfare. You may have asked "How can any of this be acts of war?" Even if God hasn't revealed every reason, it's not up to you to always understand why or how something works. *A good soldier doesn't question his orders, he just follows the command.* Make sure you are in tune with Him enough to recognize His direction.

Great Responsibility

> *"Everyone to whom much was given, of him much will be required, and from him to whom they entrusted much, they will demand the more."*
> —*Luke 12:48b*

A pastor or leader may have more to live up to. In my studies, I've found that any person claiming Christ and His power has great responsibility. Just listen to your friendly neighborhood Spiderman, "with great power comes great responsibility." Not only are we called to commit our lives as worship to God (see Romans 12:1 again), but the Bible also speaks of being above reproach. The amazing lives we live require sacrifice and honor. David wrote this in the Psalms:

> *"I will search for faithful people*
> *to be my companions.*
> *Only those who are above reproach*
> *will be allowed to serve me."*
> —*Psalms 101:6*

Purposely Placed

What do you love more: your people or your position? Strive to see people first. Each person brings giftings and skills that can supplement or complement other team members. Sometimes you'll have the same skill, but within that are idiosyncrasies and uniquenesses (it's a real word) that God wants to use.

What do you love more: your people or your position?

Sometimes people complement each other. "Nice shoes!" (No, not that kind of compliment, but it's good to establish an encouraging culture.) Often you'll challenge one another whether it be intentional or not. It's all part of God's design.

Rest in your leadership. You are where you are for a reason and a time, and the same is true for them. You may question so many aspects from their qualifications and experience to their methods and consistencies (or more likely inconsistencies). Believe me, I have, and I fight with those judgmental and arrogant tendencies as well. BUT (don't you just love a big BUT? Wait, that doesn't sound right . . .), who are you to question God's methods and reasoning?

Letting the pressure off yourself also lets the pressure off your team. When you carry the weight of success on your shoulders, others feel it as well, or may feel sorry for you. When you see that you aren't being driven by any specific person or personality, you are more willing and able to get on board, and to do so with less hesitation and fewer reservations.

> *"Honor all people, love the brotherhood, fear God, honor the king. Servants, be submissive to your masters with all respect, not only to those who are good and gentle, but also to those who are unreasonable."*
> *—1 Peter 2:17-18 (NASB)*

Attractive Leadership

> *"You attract more flies with honey than with vinegar."*
> *—Benjamin Franklin, Poor Richard's Almanac (1744)*

Be the person and leader that people want to be around

Be the person and leader that people want to be around. When you walk into a room, be the one to inspire, encourage, and infuse everyone with energy and excitement. Make it your goal to enhance every environment you enter, whether personal or professional, with sincerity, purpose and joy. Be prayed up, prepared, and proactive in the pursuit of these pleasantries. You'll have to be connected to the

Source in order to truly be effective in this. Make sure you are spending the necessary time in communion with God, seeking His wisdom, guidance, and power.

As you strive to enhance every environment you enter, consider your temper and work towards curbing your anger. Be more like honey and less like vinegar. Consider how honey pours slowly. The Bible says to "be slow to anger" (see James 1:19, Proverbs 14:29 and 15:18). While vinegar is like water, quick, terse, painful, it doesn't even have a sweet aroma. There will be a time for more direct confrontation, but it should never be in the moment or in anger. If you must, take someone aside and handle things with grace. If at all possible, try stepping back and letting others lead. In that, he or she will find his or her rhythm like you found yours; it will be beautiful to see the tribe moving together and excelling in each of their own ways, naturally finding each of their places in the symphony.

> *"The best executive is the one who has sense enough to pick good men to do what he wants done, and self-restraint enough to keep from meddling with them while they do it."*
> *—Theodore Roosevelt*
>
> *"Don't tell people how to do things, tell them what to do and let them surprise you with their results."*
> *—George S. Patton Jr.*

Subject to Change

> *"Ooh, he's in trouble!"*
> *—Something I was always afraid to hear about myself*

I recently got a 'talking-to' about being late on Sunday mornings at my campus. While I have many excuses such as communication breakdowns and life events, the real issue is that my philosophy does not currently match the leadership's philosophy. And that, in itself, is a *pride* issue. I'm aware enough to admit that some of my philosophies don't even match God's, yet. I'm working towards His ways and hope to be able to overcome my pride so that I can experience real truth in every way, the ultimate good that is God.

You should choose to trust your leadership now, so that they will trust you later

This is relevant to being a staff member, team member, or in any position under some authority. Not only is there a chance that they may know more than you do about a specific issue, but there is the matter of obedience first to God. Perhaps having a lax attitude will be good for a while but eventually could lead your team down a road that is difficult from which to return. Perhaps that way *is* the right way somewhere, someday. But its likely not here, not now. *You should choose to trust your leadership now, so that they will trust you later.* You should choose to be obedient as Christ was obedient. You should choose to submit to this authority as they ultimately submit to His authority.

> *"Therefore whoever resists the authorities resists what God has appointed, and those who resist will incur judgment. For rulers are not a terror to good conduct, but to bad. Would you have no fear of the one who is in authority? Then do what is good, and you will receive his approval, for he is God's servant for your good. But if you do wrong, be afraid, for he does not bear the sword in vain. For he is the servant of God, an avenger who carries out God's wrath on the wrongdoer. Therefore one must be in subjection, not only to avoid God's wrath but also for the sake of conscience. For because of this you also pay taxes, for the authorities are ministers of God, attending to this very thing. Pay to all what is owed to them: taxes to whom taxes are owed, revenue to whom revenue is owed, respect to whom respect is owed, honor to whom honor is owed."*
> *—Romans 13:3-7*

> *"Obey your leaders and submit to them, for they are keeping watch over your souls, as those who will have to give an account. Let them do this with joy and not with groaning, for that would be of no advantage to you. Pray for us, for we are sure that we have a clear conscience, desiring to act honorably in all things."*
> *—Hebrews 13:17-18*

Prisoner of War

One of the hardest things to navigate as a believer, and especially as a team member, is knowing how to respond when you're offended. It happens all the time in different ways, such as:

- the sound guys says you're flat or asks you to turn down your amp

- a leader confronts you on some issue

- a volunteer questions your leadership call in a situation

- you get rebuked in the middle of rehearsal or service

- someone else gets to lead "your" song: the one you usually lead

- not being invited to collaborate on a project or participate in an event/service

Most times, God has a lesson in it for you. When you get offended, remember that it is *you* who controls your emotions and chooses to be offended. Don't give that power away. Sure, hurt may be immediate, and it's hard to get that "slow to anger" bit figured out. But, *don't let your emotions take you captive, rather take captive your emotions.* You are not the prisoner here, don't act like it. Walk in freedom as you learn to deal with what you're feeling.

> *"We destroy arguments and every lofty opinion raised against the knowledge of God, and take every thought captive to obey Christ,"*
> *—2 Corinthians 10:5*

Go to God and ask Him what He wants to reveal in you. It is likely that you have some pride, jealousy, insecurity, false sense of identity, or a multitude of other such heart issues. You're not alone in that. He has something great to teach you. It's all part of that sanctification, the perfecting of your soul towards holiness.

> *"I press on toward the goal for the prize of the upward call of God in Christ Jesus. Let those of us who are mature think this way, and if in anything you think otherwise, God will reveal that also to you."*
> *—Philippians 3:13-14*

Sometimes, however, the fault will fall to the other person. If this is the case, try to have grace for them. Perhaps that team member is going through a difficult season, or maybe they don't yet realize that their leadership or servant-ship is so aggressive. This is a chance to be Christ to that person, to show love. Your humility in that moment may one day, even decades later, lead them closer to Christ in understanding as they remember how they experienced Christ's love through your actions.

You must strive to know the character of Christ as He is the ultimate example in all things. But it's hard to know when to flip the tables (John 2:15) or turn the other cheek (Luke 6:29), or when to be the lion (Revelation 5:5) or to be the lamb (John 1:29), to stand up and fight or to lay yourself down. Learn to decipher which voice is His, which is yours, and which is the enemy's. *You must be so in tune with the Holy Spirit, walking daily with Christ, pursuing the holy God, that you can recognize His guidance and His voice.* In those circumstances when you still can't figure it out, default to calm (one of our staff mottos). In this, you will be a joy to lead for your leaders, and as a leader, you will be one who can be trusted and admired for your composure and grace.

> *"Obey your leaders and submit to them, for they are keeping watch over your souls, as those who will have to give an account. Let them do this with joy and not with groaning, for that would be of no advantage to you."*
> *—Hebrew 13:17*

Hallowed Ground

The month that culminates to a controversial holiday, or un-holy-day, as some might say: Halloween, or my preference, All Hallows Eve. The earliest 'trick-or-treaters' would actually dress up and perform songs or poems for food. It sounds a bit like caroling, but with expectation, which sounds like leading worship, in a way. Stick with me here; we offer songs to people, but ultimately to God. Our expectation is not that *we* would get something out of it, but that the people would get fed in a way, or grow, or be challenged to worship.

I know, it's quite a stretch to compare Halloween to worship, but it's a good exercise to try to find a way to redeem the things of this world, just as Christ redeems the people of it. We are instructed to "take every thought captive to obey Christ" (2 Corinthians 10:5). This is especially important in times like this month when so much of the world bombards our minds unashamedly. It's like everyone feels they have a pass for reckless revelry for some reason. Don't let it fool you, lest you become the fool. Continue to offer your songs and poems to God for nourishment to your soul, and love your neighbor as best you can, better actually, with God's help.

In my song, "Hallowed Ground," I state my music's mission statement: *to speak life to the dead*. There is spiritual death all around us. As this specific season comes and goes, that will be even more evident. Anyone who does not have Christ does not have life. Just as in a graveyard, we are walking on hallowed ground with death all around us. Therefore it is of grave (see what I did there?) importance for us to speak life in everything we do communally, personally, and privately.

What you have to look forward to this month:

- The joy of your tools
- Mountaineering
- The walking faiths
- Some riddles
- A Miley Cyrus reference

Purpose in the Process

> *"Men have become the tools of their tools."*
> —*Henry David Thoreau*

As I get older, and prayerfully wiser, I find more satisfaction in the work rather than the result, the tools over the outcome, the process more than the product. Solomon understood that when he said "There is nothing better than that a man should rejoice in his work" (Ecc. 3:22). An experienced craftsman finds his true joy in working with his tools first, then in the finished product. Those that worship the product alone will lack the commitment and dedication to the craft because their passion is not fueled by the daily rigors of the work. *For it is in the making of a thing that a man finds his own making.*

> **For it is in the making of a thing that a man finds his own making**

When we use a microscope, we see what few men see. It reminds us that God sees what no man can see. It reminds us that God is the ultimate creator, the perfect designer. And we are all His tools, His workmanship; it's not any *one* of us that makes anything good, it's *every* one of us together, working for His good. He delights in our stories just as we find joy in the journey, lock in on the work, learn to embrace in the mundane, and find purpose in the process.

> *"For we are his workmanship, created in Christ Jesus for good works, which God prepared beforehand, that we should walk in them."*
> *—Ephesians 2:8-10*

Rock Climbing

We all have had a mountaintop experience of some sort:

- that camp you went to as a student or leader

- the end of a moving worship service when all the hands are raised without prompting

- the time you clearly heard from God beyond the shadow of a doubt

- the weekend event or retreat that reinvigorated your soul

- the moment in a movie when God teaches you a truth about life or reminds you of His word

- hearing your baby's first giggle

Up on this mountaintop, we can see the big picture so much more clearly; however, looking into the valley, it's hard to see all the obstacles we've overcome, and will have to overcome again on the next mountaintop charge. We often equate these experiences with the story of Moses on the mountain, when God revealed Himself to Moses whose face shone with the glory of God.

> *"When Moses came down from Mount Sinai, with the two tablets of the testimony in his hand as he came down from the mountain, Moses did not know that the skin of his face shone because he had been talking with God."*
> *—Exodus 34:29*

We all wish we could stay on the mountaintop or jump straight to the next one; but no one lives mountaintop to mountaintop without going through the valleys. That's part of the journey. It's also part of what makes each mountaintop such an exceptional experience. The mountaintop adventure is so much better when we've had to go through a valley and a grueling climb, each step harder than the last.

If you were just dropped off up there by helicopter, sure, it'd be amazing; it would still be one of the greatest experiences of your life. But you wouldn't be a mountaineer. When you have climbed for days to reach that summit, there is something deeper in you than most will ever experience. You will have achieved something that transcends explanation.

I've never climbed a mountain, but I've ridden motorcycles. If I were to try to explain riding a motorcycle, you wouldn't really get it. Only after you've done it will you get it; then, we'll share an unspoken bond, partly because we've both been there and partly because neither of us can find the words to truly describe it. The only way to know it is to have experienced it.

> *"There comes the baffling call of God in our lives also. The call of God can never be stated explicitly, it is implicit. The call of God is like the call of the sea, no one hears it but the one who has the nature of the sea in him. It cannot be stated definitely what the call of God is to, because his call is to be in comradeship with himself for his own purposes, and the test is to believe that God knows what he is after."*
> *—Oswald Chambers*

Faith Walks

> *"Brother, the grass grows on your path."*
> —*Early African converts*

Early African converts to Christianity had dedicated paths that led to sacred places where each of them spent time with God. Do you have a place for your devotional time with God? Do you have a specified private worship time for Him? For some it's a closet, for others an actual path on which they walk. For most of us, it's wherever we can make it work: in the car, an impromptu walk around the church or park, a bathroom stall (don't act like you don't have pre-service 'time with God.' Sometimes it's the only time and place for it).

Make time for Him before time is required of you

Before your brother has to ask you, ask yourself if grass is growing on your path. Go on a faith walk. Go to a prayer closet. Go to the bathroom (you know what I mean!). *Make time for Him before time is required of you.* Get alone with God in a consistent way. Additionally, faith doesn't sit still. Faith walks: it moves, it acts, it requires the breath of God, His very word, Christ Himself.

> *"So faith comes from hearing, and hearing through the word of Christ."*
> —*Romans 10:17*

Hold Fast and Press On

I love riddles.

One of my best friends, a young man of faith, wit, and will, was in a philosophy class when the teacher tried to stump him.

The professor asked, "Can God create a door that opens and closes at the same time?"

My friend thought about it and, in true philosophical fashion, answered with this question, "What about a revolving door?"

Much like the conflicting idea of a door opening and closing, sometimes, in our minds, the logic of God seems oxymoronic, like a riddle. Yet, we encounter oxymoron-like commands: *hold* fast and *press* on, *fight* and *lay down* your life, *stand* firm and *run* the race. These things are sometimes commanded in different contexts, but occasionally at the same time. How can two seemingly opposing things be our simultaneous instruction? Occasionally, we need to look deeper, but more often, we need to trust that God is bigger and has a way.

> *"For my thoughts are not your thoughts,*
> *neither are your ways my ways, declares the Lord.*
> *For as the heavens are higher than the earth,*
> *so are my ways higher than your ways*
> *and my thoughts than your thoughts."*
> *—Isaiah 55:8-9*

> *"Oh, the depth of the riches both of the wisdom and knowledge of God! How unsearchable are His judgments and unfathomable His ways!"*
> *—Romans 11:33 (NASB)*

- Hold fast and press on: perhaps it's the helm of a ship, the steering wheel of a car, a baton being passed, the grindstone of a mill house
- Fight and lay down your life: this one makes sense for any of you who have lost a loved one in the military or who recognize how Christ chose His battles
- Stand firm and run the race: either way, plant each foot firmly in faith

If you can't settle yourself, try allowing God to calm your soul

Settle yourself. *If you can't settle yourself, try allowing God to calm your soul.* Instead of trying to work out His logic, lean into faith and let the Holy Spirit guide you. You'll find that the answers are much simpler than you expected. Sometimes you won't find the answers; by then, you won't need them.

Hands Up, They're Playing My Song

> *"Lift up your hands to the holy place and bless the Lord!"*
> *—Psalms 132:2*

Here are some useful prompts for raising hands, should you so desire to share:

- Have you ever had a child run up to you? Maybe he's fallen and gotten hurt, or maybe he's just excited to see you. What does he do? He looks up, calls you a name of endearment, and raises his hands for you to pick him up. Whether you're hurt or just glad to see God, look to your Father, and ask Him to pick you up out of your pain and to hold you.

- In a battle, at the moment of surrender, what do the losing warriors do? What is the universal sign of surrender? Raising hands. If you've had all you can take and are ready to give up control of your life to God, to surrender to His will for your life, a will and plan for amazing things that you could never even dream of, then raise your hands to Him. Allow that first act of obedience to set the stage for all that follows.

- Raising your hands makes you vulnerable, exposing your core to those around with no means of protection. It opens your heart to whatever may come. It also shows that you have nothing to hide, or shows what you have been hiding. It is a massive act of trust, basically putting your life in the hands of the one in front of you. Use this challenge to grow your faith in God, to allow Him to get close. He will bring healing to your wounds, He will mend your heart, He will wrap you in His loving arms. He is not to be feared as an enemy, for He is your Father, your Creator, your Friend, your Defender, your Savior, your true Love.

- In joy! Triumphantly! When your team wins, what do you do? You and the entire stadium go crazy for every victory. You've donned you war-paint and now raise your hands in triumph: past, present, or potential!

- Simply enough, in obedience and praise. By example, we follow the psalmists and our biblical mentors from the multitude, the plethora, if you will, of verses throughout the written Word of God. (Could this *be* any more spiritual? Methinks not.)

grATTITUDE

The month of giving thanks seems to be intentionally placed just after the day of giving 'no cares'. Course correction possibly? Or maybe it's preparation for the next month when we *give* under the guise of generosity. The truth is that gratitude and generosity go hand in hand.

When you are given something, big or small, you say, "Thank you." As creatives, singers, musicians, and Christians, our "thank you" comes out as worship. As you remember from earlier, worship is life. So gratitude is more of a lifestyle than a momentary choice.

> **It is gratitude, like worship, that recognizes that we aren't responsible for making good the thing that is happening in front of us**

It is gratitude, like worship, that recognizes that we aren't responsible for making good the thing that is happening in front of us. It is gratitude that shifts our perspective to its proper place. It is gratitude that takes the weight from our talents and plans when we see that someone else has it covered, when we see that God is really in control.

Thanksgiving is really another facet of worship, so let your life be one of thanksgiving, not just for that week or month, but consistently. It will help relieve so much more than you know. Not only do you get the initial gifts for which you are thankful, but you will continue to be gifted in understanding and peace. Continue to return those gifts to God, and thrive in His presence.

What you have to look forward to this month:

- God's perseverance
- Your worthiness
- The synonymous-ness of grace and praise
- Moon language

Empty

> *"Hunger is just emptiness that someone doesn't understand."*
> *—Heroes Reborn*

Do you sometimes feel you're running on empty? That means you are hungry. If you are hungry, you haven't been eating, or at least not eating enough. You feel empty because you need spiritual sustenance. You feel tired because you have been working for man and not for God. You feel exhausted because your focus is not right.

Yes, you need rest, but you need God first. You need righteousness, Christ Himself, flowing through you, renewing you in every moment, every day, every circumstance and situation. You need the constant breath of life, the consistent bread of life, what He alone can truly offer and fulfill. *You may face fatigue that overwhelms, so remember that God does not grow weary.*

> *"Jesus said to them, 'I am the bread of life; whoever comes to me shall not hunger, and whoever believes in me shall never thirst.'"*
> *—John 6:35*

"Come to me, all who labor and are heavy laden, and I will give you rest. Take my yoke upon you, and learn from me, for I am gentle and lowly in heart, and you will find rest for your souls. For my yoke is easy, and my burden is light."
—Matthew 11:28-30

Unworthy

Do you ever question whether you are worthy of the great opportunities in front of you? Whether it be on the stage or just standing with other believers in service, we have all felt like we didn't deserve to be there. The truth is, you're right, kind of.

> *"for all have sinned and fall short of the glory of God."*
> —*Romans 3:23*

You are not worthy, no one is. But Christ, who lives within you, He is worthy. When you feel you don't deserve to be there, on stage serving or in the congregation worshiping, you're right. But thank God that He doesn't leave you alone with your unrighteous self. He sent His son to be worthy for you. And since you have Christ, and He lives in you, then you are made righteous. You can be used where you are. Not because of you or anything you've done, but purely because of the atonement of Christ who suffered the penalty for our sins.

Don't insult the power of His blood by continuing to think that you don't deserve to be where you are, serving Him and His kingdom. He calls you a saint, and has saved you by grace. *You are not your worst moments,* you are not defined by those things anymore.

> You are not your worst moments, you are not defined by those things anymore

You are not a *sinner* saved by grace. You are a saint! You are a child of the King! That is your name, that is your heritage, that is your identity!

> *"He himself bore our sins in his body on the tree, that we might die to sin and live to righteousness. By his wounds you have been healed"*
> *—1 Peter 2:24*

> *"For if the blood of bulls and goats and the ashes of a heifer, sprinkling the unclean, sanctifies for the purifying of the flesh, how much more shall the blood of Christ, who through the eternal Spirit offered Himself without spot to God, cleanse your conscience from dead works to serve the living God?"*
> *—Hebrews 9:13-14*

Grace to Praise

If you are breathing, then God still has purpose for you. Each breath you take is a reminder of that, to live another day in order that you might bring more glory to God and do His kingdom work. That is a grace that you, the living, have each waking moment. So it is fair to say that you are breathing in His grace with each inhalation, each recollection of air, each expansion of your lungs.

What better way to spend that grace, that very same breath, than in worship, than to breathe it out as praise? This is what you are meant to do! This is your natural rhythm. You are made to worship, to convert what He gives into what He gets.

> **You are breathing in His grace and breathing out His praise!**

You are breathing in His grace and breathing out His praise! Take that very same breath that reminds you that you have a purpose, and use it for that very purpose: to glorify God!

"Praise the Lord!
Praise God in his sanctuary;
praise him in his mighty heavens!
Praise him for his mighty deeds;
praise him according to his excellent greatness!
Praise him with trumpet sound;
praise him with lute and harp!
Praise him with tambourine and dance;
praise him with strings and pipe!
Praise him with sounding cymbals;
praise him with loud clashing cymbals!
Let everything that has breath praise the Lord!
Praise the Lord!"
—Psalms 150: 1-6

Moon People

Here is some interesting language: "increasingly formed into His image as we prepare for our eternal home with Him. Everything else pales in comparison." Am I the only one who thinks this kind of language sounds like some crazy person who believes in moon people? (If you do believe in moon people by chance, I don't *necessarily* think you're crazy, but you can see how it sounds, right?) Sometimes when you start speaking your jargon (another strange word for words), you alienate those around you who haven't caught up to the vernacular.

> *"But we are citizens of heaven, where the Lord Jesus Christ lives. And we are eagerly waiting for him to return as our Savior."*
> *—Philippians 3:20*

Listen to how that can sound: we are just visitors here. (Insert alien voice) "Earth is not our home, our true resting place." It's all true, but how strange it must be to so many people new to church. As we see more new people coming into the church, we should take Paul's advice when he says to be "all things to all people" (NIV).

Our leadership, passion, and trust in God is all on display in a new way

This is especially appropriate for Thanksgiving weekend when we see a lot of new faces, visitors from foreign lands who've come to break bread and devour meat with people they call family.

While numbers may feel low this weekend, the ratio of visitors to members is staggeringly high. As stale as the emptier environment can feel, it is brand new to so many there. *Our leadership, passion, and trust in God is all on display in a new way.*

So this Thanksgiving, and as the holiday season gets into full swing, let's not be moon people to the earthlings. Let's save that language for our moon people gatherings. We should try not to speak Christianese as it may segregate. However, we can always speak the universal languages that God puts forth: love, hope, peace, joy, and more.

> *"I have become all things to all men, so that by all means I might save some."*
> *—1 Corinthians 9:22*

Merry X-mas!

December is about one thing: Christmas! Fun fact, some people think that calling it X-mas is removing 'Christ' from Christmas, but it actually isn't. X is the Greek letter "chi" and is used as a substitute for "Christ," so there you go. Even when the world has its plans, God's are bigger.

X-mas is about Jesus, but it also brings insane busyness that can kill the very spirits that are trying to be lifted in this season. Maybe that's part of it all, knowing the season is heavy causes us to act as though it isn't. We're stretched, but there are bigger reasons to endure.

We will grow in this time, and we will have to lean on Christ. We will need 'mas' Christ this Christmas, *more* of Christ. *It is through the hardest times in life that we have the sweetest times with Christ.* Don't miss the beauty in the chaos.

> It is through the hardest times in life that we have the sweetest times with Christ

Just like having children, it's overwhelming and easy to look ahead for the next breather, the next milestone. But in doing so, you aren't watching what's happening in the in-between moments, not like you'll wish you had. When the storm is over, your focus shifts quickly to rest, recovery, and rebuilding. After the craziness and a bit of time, you'll look forward to the next go-around, but it will never be the same again. Each of you has changed.

The future is full of variables: people will cycle through your life, cultures will change, society will transform, things will be different. You'll never have this experience again with these people at this time with these challenges. You must strive to not miss it, or you will.

What you have to look forward to this month:

- Family mentality

- Having more than you can handle

- How to worship without a promise

- The salvation of kings

Competition

Without competition, it's possible that there would be no Olympians, fantastic sporting events, technological advances, vast medical achievements, ambition, or even progress as a society. For some people, there would be no reason for living. How sad is it that the world lives that way? We compete for stage time, for admiration and influence, for respect and attention. We all do, Christians as well, maybe more so in some cases.

> *"Then I saw that all toil and all skill in work come from a man's envy of his neighbor. This also is vanity and a striving after wind . . . his eyes are never satisfied with riches, so that he never asks, "For whom am I toiling and depriving myself of pleasure?" This also is vanity and an unhappy business. Two are better than one, because they have a good reward for their toil . . . a threefold cord is not quickly broken."*
> *—Ecclesiastes 4:4,8b-12*

A majority of studies in the field of competition have shown that *cooperation promotes higher achievement than competition*. This may seem a surprise to the world, but it's been this way in God's kingdom and hierarchy since the beginning. When Satan tried to compete with God, he was immediately removed. God, the Son, and the Holy Spirit operate in harmony and complement each other. There is no competition, nor is there room for it.

We are family: the global church, your congregation, your team. When one of us succeeds, we should all rejoice with that person. We are all messengers, all heralds of the King; therefore, we all have equal shares. When someone does well, we can celebrate that person because we're really celebrating the message of Christ and the grace of our God.

> *"Care more that He just speaks. We survive on what He says . . . so it doesn't matter who He is speaking through, just that He speaks."*
> —*Steffany Gretzinger (paraphrased)*

Strengthen My Hands

> *"I was pushed hard, so that I was falling, but the Lord helped me."*
> *Psalms 118:13*

It's a busy time. I don't even know you, but I know you're maxed out. The church has functions, rehearsals, parties, and events. Your families are pulling you different directions. If you work outside of the church, or bi-vocationally like myself, then your jobs are likely expanding your responsibilities. You are trying to maintain friendships and hobbies through this time as well. Then, there are kids! Or more likely, they've come first in most of this. Rest? Well, you take rest when you can get it.

You've heard it said, "It's a season, it'll pass." I've been in that *season* for over two years! Sometimes life doesn't change. It's you that has to change, adapt, grow stronger, and become wiser. You learn to lean on God more and more until you walk in His strength daily. He wants to use you in every capacity in which you're capable and more!

> He will allow you to be in over your head so that you learn to reach out for Him

The old saying, "God will never give you more than you can handle," is ridiculous! If that were true, why would we ever need Him? *He will allow you to be in over your head so that you learn to reach out for Him*, so that you learn how to access His strength, so that you learn how to walk with His Spirit.

"For they all wanted to frighten us, thinking, 'Their hands will drop from the work, and it will not be done.' But now, O God, strengthen my hands.'"
—Nehemiah 6:10

"What gain has the worker from his toil? I have seen the business that God has given to the children of man to be busy with. He has made everything beautiful in its time. Also, he has put eternity into man's heart, yet so that he cannot find out what God has done from the beginning to the end. I perceived that there is nothing better for them than to be joyful and to do good as long as they live; also that everyone should eat and drink and take pleasure in all his toil—this is God's gift to man."
—Ecclesiastes 3:9-13

His Terms

Let's recount the story of Paul and Silas in prison and the amazing picture of the power of praise in dire circumstances:

> *"About midnight Paul and Silas were praying and singing hymns to God, and the prisoners were listening to them, and suddenly there was a great earthquake, so that the foundations of the prison were shaken. And immediately all the doors were opened, and everyone's bonds were unfastened."*
> —Act 16:23-26

When it says, "about midnight," it reads as if they had been praising God for hours. As it goes, they weren't seeking rescue. They had a chance to leave. As far as we can tell, they were purely and simply seeking God and glorifying Him for who He is, not for what He was doing.

They didn't seem desperate or worried even though they had been beaten and disrespected. They weren't praising Him in hopes that *their* tasks would be fulfilled. They weren't worshiping Him because it was what's expected. They weren't singing hymns to God to impress the other prisoners listening to them. They weren't praying for a Savior for the moment. They were simply walking in their purpose, glorifying God, and reaching out to Him because they loved Him.

There *happened to be* an earthquake that shook the foundations of those around them. There *happened to be* shackles loosed. There *happened to be* a move of God that led to salvation, life change, and redemption.

How many times do we use this story to motivate worshipers? That's great! Keep doing it! God *will* change lives, bring salvation, and redeem! However, it won't always be on our terms. We must learn to worship Him regardless of what He is doing. *We must learn to praise a Savior for the simple magnificent fact that He is the Savior.* We must acquire the mindset of Christ to empty ourselves, taking the form of servants (see Phil. 2:5-7). We must pour ourselves into worship without the promise of deliverance from our current bonds.

> The best of us is Christ, in Him, through Him, and for Him

Our best does not require or merit His best. For it is the ultimate salvation that we already have, the promise that this world does not nor ever will have the best of us. And *the best of us is Christ, in Him, through Him, and for Him.*

God Save the Queen

I bet you thought I'd make this political, or maybe evangelical: God save the Queen, and the rest of the world! Nope, it's just click-bait, or more like flip-bait.

If you invited the president or the queen over, you would spend a lot of time, and maybe even money, preparing for it. When a church has larger events, such as Easter or Christmas, it goes all out to make it as impactful as possible.

Do not take your preparation lightly. This is war

But how much time do you spend prepping to invite God to move on a regular basis? Do not take your leadership and responsibility lightly. *Do not take your preparation lightly. This is war.*

Okay, that got really heavy, really quick. It's simple though. If you will value the Spirit of God as you would a prominent public figure, then invest, whether it's a light show and fog machines, or time spent in public expectation, or private worship.

> *"Yet you are holy, enthroned on the praises of Israel."*
> —*Psalms 22:3*

One of the most common correlations to powerful events is expectation. God moves in faith and expectation. Or better yet, He is able to move more efficiently due to our willingness to have Him move. God inhabits our praises: when we sing to Him, He is here, dwelling in that praise, living in it, and filling the room. However, it is not our praise that draws Him out, rather it is our openness to His workings that give us more access to who He is and what He offers!

For the record, I do hope that God saves all of the queens, kings, dukes, earls, dukes of earls, and peasants alike.

Final Charge:
Keep Fighting

You may be a year in, a day in, or a lifetime in service at this point. New recruits are coming in daily, and former friends and allies have fallen, some never to fight again, having been raised to glory with God. Some have just fallen away, running away in desertion or turning against God. Arguably, some of them never even knew Him to begin with. *How could anyone who has truly tasted the glory of God ever turn from Him?* Yet, it still seems to happen. The enemy is good at what he does. He's been at it for thousands of years. Don't be naive. You are not above his temptations. Continue to sharpen your weapons, increase your arsenal, and seek battle plans from on high. You are not alone in this fight, but you alone carry the responsibility of following through with your orders. God has no faults, makes no mistakes, and has already unleashed the perfect battle plan for victory: His son. The war is already won. If you continue to rely on Him, you can walk in that victory every time you choose to worship Him in the midst of the battle.

> *"Fight the good fight of the faith. Take hold of the eternal life to which you were called and about which you made the good confession in the presence of many witnesses."*
> *—1 Timothy 6:12*

Back Pocket Devos

110 Percent

You've heard the old encouragement, "Give it a hundred and ten percent!" Being a math person, and just a logical human being, those sayings have always bothered me. It's not possible to give over one hundred percent of yourself! You are only physically made up of precisely one hundred percent, and it's very difficult to call upon that as is.

In recent seasons of busyness and uncertainty of direction, I've heard or felt what I believe to be a challenge from God: give 100% to whatever is in front of you. I've never really felt like that was even possible. But He challenged me to do it from task to task, job to job, calling to calling. So I put forth my best effort. Then I do it again for the next task. I don't know if I ever give a full 100%, but I've given 80% and watched Him provide the extra 20%. *He is ready and willing to compensate for our lack when we trust Him to do so.* If I do give 100%, He may choose to add 10%, which equals . . . you guessed it: something impossible. Maybe it's not possible, but since when does God operate by our rules? It is *possible* (however you define that term) when you let God provide. He is the God of your impossibilities.

> *"I can do all things through Christ who strengthens me."*
> *—Philippians 4:13*

You Are Not Alone

> *"Praise the LORD! Sing to the LORD a new song,*
> *His praise in the assembly of the godly!"*
> *—Psalms 149:1*

Obviously, God is with you. Dive into His Word if you are unsure of His presence. Other than His constant presence, you are still not alone. *You're not the only one putting his or her whole heart into the service.* You have other team members doing so. If you don't recognize that, know that another church down the road or across the country has someone like you, pressing forward and running the race with reckless abandon!

Our church currently has three campuses doing the same set list at similar times every Sunday morning; it's amazing to think of our people across the county singing simultaneous praises to God. Now, imagine all the other churches in your area, singing some theme of praise or worship to our great God. It goes on from there! Across the region, state, country, and world, people are singing of God and to Him, worshiping as one church. What a beautiful picture!

"And when the priests came out of the Holy Place (for all the priests who were present had consecrated themselves, without regard to their divisions . . . and it was the duty of the trumpeters and singers to make themselves heard in unison in praise and thanksgiving to the LORD), and when the song was raised, with trumpets and cymbals and other musical instruments, in praise to the LORD"
—2 Chronicles 5:11, 13

"After this I looked, and behold, a great multitude that no one could number, from every nation, from all tribes and peoples and languages, standing before the throne and before the Lamb, clothed in white robes, with palm branches in their hands, and crying out with a loud voice, "Salvation belongs to our God who sits on the throne, and to the Lamb!"
—Revelation 7:9-10

Repurposers

We, as musicians, artists, technological enthusiasts, and creatives, often think of our work as our creation. There is danger in calling ourselves creators. We like to think we come up with new things, but the verse above speaks to the contrary. So can we create something?

Recently, I was so excited to teach about creativity and passions for an upcoming event, so I began to share some of my thoughts with my wife. If you ever need to be challenged, go to your significant other. My wife is the string to my kite, and I thank God for her. I told her that since we are created in God's image, and He is the creator of the universe, then we are creators. She told me to be careful with that thought. I said, "Well, you are creating life inside of you right now" (she was early in her first pregnancy), to which she replied, "No, God created this child. I am just helping to foster that life." That messed up my view, not to mention the teaching point! So I consider us to be something different. Yes, we are crea*tive*, but we don't *create* in the way that God creates.

God is the sole Creator of all things; *we* participate in the rearrangement of existent things. Did I create these songs I've written or were they gifts from God for His purpose and design? What if the song isn't to glorify

God? Did I create it then? Well, arguably, I just took similar words, chords, melodies, and more and *repurposed* them into a new (to someone) arrangement. Does woman create life with the help of man? No, she simply fosters it. Her body provides for it, but God initiated that life and as the Psalm says, He 'forms' each life in the mother's womb.

We are *Repurposers*. Isn't that also an attribute of God? He takes a sinful man and redeems Him through the blood of Christ, He restores and renews that man into a new creation, one that is being made to glorify Himself, the Creator.

You have the ability to creatively put things together in interesting and meaningfully ways. *Your service is unique in the ways that God Himself is involved.* Be encouraged by this perspective: you don't carry the weight of creating, God has done that already. You simply need to let Him guide you into repurposing what you know and have experienced into something that honors Him.

Good Band Etiquette

When someone messes up or something goes wrong, make sure to:

- Stare directly at the person at fault
- Make the strangest face you can muster
- Laugh (too loudly)—a smile is bound to appear though, often from multiple members
- Stop the set and yell at the musician, throwing a tantrum and your instrument simultaneously (I've actually seen variations of this)

Please note my sarcasm and candor. Chances are, most people don't even notice the mistakes. Those who did will usually have grace. However, those who noticed and let you know that they noticed are actually potential volunteers! If they have that skill set musically and such attention to detail, then ask if they would like to audition or serve in some capacity!

When a moment falls flat or a transition feels awkward, definitely follow these guidelines:

- Stare a hole through the back of the worship leader's head

- Fumble with your pedals or gear as if something is "broken" or "not-working"

- Decide to play an impromptu doodle to "ease" the moment

It's likely that those moments aren't nearly as awkward or lengthy as you think. Time feels different when you're on the stage or operating equipment. It speeds up or slows down relative to the moments and your anxiety. Remember that there can be beauty in the silence. Just like in a painting, white space, or blank space, is just as valuable or more so as any color you put on the canvas. A moment of silence can guide an atmosphere to a new dimension. Rest in the remission.

Such things happen embarrassingly too often in our church services. Overall though, it's one moment in one weekend when you've done all you can do in preparation. Sometimes the enemy gets involved. Sometimes you give the enemy too much credit, and it's a simple malfunction that serves as a learning opportunity. Sometimes God has a plan that's bigger than ours (see "Even If We Crash and Burn"). *Don't play the blame game, just recognize, course correct, and press on!*

Let the Hungry Dwell Here

"For he satisfies the longing soul,
and the hungry soul he fills with good things."
—Psalms 107:9

Am I satisfied with Jesus? I chase so many other things that 'satisfy' me. What if I was just satisfied with Him? I want this to be my heart:

"As a deer pants for flowing streams,
so pant my soul for you, O God.
My soul thirsts for God,
for the living God."
—Psalms 42:1-2a

Get your eyes off the things of this world. They do nothing but create starvation that you didn't have before. You are perfectly content with your car until you start looking at others'. Then you feel you deserve something new, or at least different; you yearn for something that you didn't yearn for before. It's a vicious downward spiral. When you take your focus off that thing, it loosens its hold on you. When you put your focus on something truly holy, nothing can tear you away. Purposes become clear, motivation becomes pure, hope is found, love flows through you, peace inexplicably surrounds you, and joy abounds within you in ways you have long since forgotten. You have a new sense of wonder, a new perspective that exposes the world's poorly polished imitation brass by putting it next to real, untarnished gold.

Give Him your undivided attention so that you will remain undivided from Him. Don't be like a glow-in-the-dark object that charges up for an hour only to last a few minutes without the light source. Carry His light with you, draw from it constantly. The dullness of that which is currently around you begs for the presence of God, which exists in you. You are charged to carry Him to those lifeless places. You are charged with an eternal power source because it doesn't rest in the ground, at home, or in transformers and power lines along the roads. It is inside you, constantly renewing and expanding. Stay connected to Him, and He will provide your paths clearly. *When you hunger for Him, partake, and you will always be satisfied.*

"O God, you are my God; earnestly I seek you;
my soul thirsts for you;
my flesh faints for you,
as in a dry and weary land where there is no water.
So I have looked upon you in the sanctuary,
beholding your power and glory.
Because your steadfast love is better than life,
my lips will praise you.
So I will bless you as long as I live;
in your name I will lift up my hands.
My soul will be satisfied as with fat and rich food,
and my mouth will praise you with joyful lips,
when I remember you upon my bed,
and meditate on you in the watches of the night;
for you have been my help,
and in the shadow of your wings I will sing for joy.
My soul clings to you;
your right hand upholds me."
—Psalms 63:1-8

URGENT REQUEST

Thank You for Reading This Book!

I'd love to hear your thoughts and need your help to make the next version (and future books) better!

Please leave *an honest, insightful review on Amazon* for others to consider this book.

If you have specific suggestions that you feel will benefit other worshipers, please contact me at aswefightbook.com/contact *after* you leave your review!

Godspeed!
— Michael Lacey

ACKNOWLEDGEMENTS

At risk of sounding like an acceptance speech, I want to thank:

God for His constant guidance and infusion of passions into my life.

My mother who always encouraged me to write, sing, and chase dreams. Her vigor for life is truly unmatched, and that is one thing from her that I hope I always carry with me.

My wife for the ways that she challenges me, both positive and negative, which help to make me a better man.

My friends who spent time over the holidays reading and sharing thoughts on the first draft: Travis, Paige, Frankie, Steve, Daniel, Drew, and Josh

Self-Publishing School for the tools and motivation to get this book done and out there!

REFERENCES

Scripture:

"BibleGateway." *BibleGateway.com: A Searchable Online Bible in over 150 Versions and 50 Languages.* N.p., n.d. Web.

Scripture quotations marked (NKJV) are taken from the New King James Version®. Copyright © 1982 by Thomas Nelson. Used by permission. All rights reserved.

Scripture quotations marked (NLT) are taken from the New Living Translation®. Copyright © 1996, 2004, 2007 by Tyndale House Publishers. Used by permission. All rights reserved.

Scripture quotations marked (NIV) are taken from the Holy Bible, New International Version®, NIV®. Copyright © 1973, 1978, 1984, 2011 by Biblica, Inc.™ Used by permission of Zondervan. All rights reserved worldwide. www.zondervan.com The "NIV" and "New International Version" are trademarks registered in the United States Patent and Trademark Office by Biblica, Inc.™

From Preface:

May, Rollo. "What Is Courage?" *The Courage to Create*. Toronto: Bantam, 1976. N. pag. Print.

From Fight I:

February:

Week 4:

Miller, Stephen. "We Are Artists." *Worship Leaders: We Are Not Rock Stars*. Chicago: Moody, 2013. N. pag. Print.

From Fight II:

April:

Franklin, Benjamin, and Carl Japikse. *Fart Proudly: Writings of Benjamin Franklin You Never Read in School*. Columbus, OH: Enthea, 1990. Print.

Week 2:

Conrad, Patrick. Sermon, *Holidazed Week 3*. https://vimeo.com/193257603.

May:

Week 1:

Eldredge, John. *Wild at Heart*. Nashville, TN: Thomas Nelson, 2006. Print.

Week 3:

Society, National Geographic. "Planet." *National Geographic Society*. N.p., 09 Oct. 2012. Web. 01 Feb. 2017.

June:

Week 3:

McManus, Erwin Raphael. "Crash the Future." *The Barbarian Way: Unleash the Untamed Faith within*. Nashville, TN: Nelson, 2005. N. pag. Print.

From Fight III:

July

Fifth Week:

Gurnall, William, and James S. Bell. *The Christian in Complete Armour: Daily Readings in Spiritual Warfare*. Chicago: Moody, 1994. Print.

August:

August Rush. Perf. Robin Williams. N.p., n.d. Web.

Week 3:

The Secret Life of Walter Mitty. Dir. Ben Stiller. Twentieth Century Fox, 2013. Film.

From Fight IV:

"Poor Richard's Almanack, 1744." *Benjamin Franklin | AMDOCS: Documents for the Study of American History*. George Laughead, Lynn H. Nelson, n.d. Web. 14 Dec. 2016.

October:

Https://www.facebook.com/JournalistAmyWillis. "Halloween 2016: History behind All Hallow's Eve and Why We Celebrate the Date." *Metro*. N.p., 28 Oct. 2016. Web. 12 Dec. 2016.

Week 2:

> Chambers, Oswald. *My Utmost for His Highest*. Uhlrichsville, OH: Barbour, 1997. Print.

Week 3:

> "The Grass Grows on Your Path." *The Grass Grows on Your Path | Ministry127*. N.p., n.d. Web. 28 Nov. 2016.

Fifth Week:

> Cyrus, Miley. *Can't Be Tamed*. Hollywood Records, 2010. CD.

November

Week 1:

> *Heroes Reborn*. N.d. Television Series. 2015.

December:

Week 1:

"No Contest: The Case against Competition", by Alfie Kohn (book Review), Share International Archives. *No Contest: The Case against Competition, by Alfie Kohn (book Review), Share International Archives.* N.p., n.d. Web. 20 Nov. 2016.

Youtube. "Bethel Interview." Online video clip. *Youtube*, currently unlisted. Web.

ABOUT THE AUTHOR

Michael Lacey, the worship leader at the West campus of Life Fellowship Church in Walls, MS, has been leading and studying worship since 2006. Passionate about leading people to a deeper connection with God through musical worship, Michael strives to inspire and build up team members who want to seek the face of God in worship both privately and in corporate settings. A devoted husband to Ashton, also a worship leader; and father to Nathan, a future musician, Michael feels privileged to serve with his family at church. He is a man of many interests and gifts, much to his wife's dismay, including motorcycles, amateur wood-working, teaching and tutoring Math, songwriting, and obviously book writing. As he wholeheartedly chases after the dreams God has placed in his heart, he keeps one eye on the horizon for what is next.

SELF-PUBLISHING
SCHOOL

NOW IT'S YOUR TURN

Discover the EXACT 3-step blueprint you need to become a bestselling author in 3 months.

Self-Publishing School helped me,
and now I want them to help you with this
FREE VIDEO SERIES!

Even if you're busy, bad at writing, or don't know where to start, you CAN write a bestseller and build your best life.

With tools and experience across a variety niches and professions, Self-Publishing School is the <u>only</u> resource you need to take your book to the finish line!

DON'T WAIT

Watch this FREE VIDEO SERIES now, and

Say "YES" to becoming a bestseller:

GO TO WRITETIME.ML FOR THE FIRST VIDEO